THE VOICE OF THE SAINTS

"For out of the abundance of the heart the mouth speaketh."

Matthew 12:34

THE VOICE
OF THE SAINTS

*Counsels from the Saints
to bring comfort and guidance
in daily living*

Selected and Arranged by
FRANCIS W. JOHNSTON

*"The mouth of the just shall bring
forth wisdom."*
Proverbs 10:31

TAN BOOKS AND PUBLISHERS, INC.
Rockford, Illinois 61105

NIHIL OBSTAT

Antverpiæ, 2 Martii 1965

Fl. Van der Veken, S.J., libr. cens.

IMPRIMATUR

Antverpiæ, 2 Martii 1965

C. Eykens, Vic. Gen.

Library of Congress Catalog Card No.: 86-50851

ISBN: 0-89555-304-X

Printed and bound in the United States of America.

TAN BOOKS AND PUBLISHERS, INC.

P.O. Box 424

Rockford, Illinois 61105

1986

TO

MARY

THE MOTHER OF GOD,

QUEEN OF ALL SAINTS

AND

HELP OF CHRISTIANS

PREFACE

WHEN we reflect on the doctrine of the Communion of Saints, with its common bond of union binding together all members of the Church in this world and the next, including all honest seekers after God (who may be designated members of the Church by desire), we are at once conscious of the wonderful unity and harmony of Christ's Mystical Body. Through the Communion of Saints there flows ceaselessly from Christ, who is the Head, grace and spiritual riches to all the members of His Mystical Body. We share in all the virtues and merits of the Saints. What belongs to one belongs to all. "Everything good which the Saints ever brought about", explains St Thomas Aquinas, "is imparted to those who live in Charity, because they are all one."

Further consideration of this wonderful Mystery of Faith leads us to the realization that we can even share in the very lives of the Saints. All their hard-won experience gained in surmounting the most stubborn difficulties and frustrations of life, in sustaining an extraordinary variety of trials, in ultimately beating down the most persistent temptations—all this wealth of experience has been handed down by the Saints as a rich legacy for us to assume. Their counsels are the fruit of triumphant living. Together with the shining example of their holy lives, they form a perfect complement to the stream of spiritual riches which we receive from them through the Communion of Saints.

It is the purpose of this book to present the substance of these counsels.

This work lays no claim to being a comprehensive treasury of the wisdom and words of the Saints. Nor does it include all those sayings that have become known for their poetry or facility of expression. These are the teachings of the Saints which, I feel, exercise a powerful influence upon our daily lives, directing us in the most important undertaking we are called upon to perform—the fulfilment of our spiritual duties.

When the plan of this work was first conceived, it was immediately evident that a formidable research would be necessary. All the available writings of the Saints that I could come across, including their letters, sermons and sayings, had to be closely scrutinized. The quotations in this book were therefore compiled from an incredible variety of sources. Besides the standard works, which I have acknowledged elsewhere, my sources included countless books and booklets, most of which have been long out of print, old manuscripts, ecclesiastical tomes dating back to the last century, numberless religious magazines, pamphlets and prayer cards, all fed by a steady stream of material from various religious houses in North America and Europe.

It would be impossible therefore to compile an accurate bibliography.

That I was able to accomplish so much is a splendid tribute to the co-operation of many kind helpers.

First, I must express my thanks to the staff of the Vancouver Catholic Library for their generous help in locating many required volumes. Thanks are also due to the Basilian Fathers, Vancouver, for permission to use the facilities of St Mark's Library, University of British Columbia; to Reverend Francis Lawless, C.SS.R., for use of the Redemptorist Fathers' private library in Vancouver, which I found particularly helpful; to the Augustinian Fathers for use of their library at the Monastery of Our Lady of Consolation, Ladner, B.C.; and finally, to the Benedictine Fathers of Westminster Abbey, Mission City, B.C., who gave me much assistance in utilizing the resources of their splendid library and kindly permitted me to reside at the Monastery for the duration of my research there.

I am also indebted to Reverend Francis X. Chang and Reverend J.L. Lemire, S.S.S., of the Archdiocese of Vancouver, B.C., for assistance in research. Also to Miss Patricia Young, the well-known Canadian Catholic author and columnist, and Mr. Andrew F. O'Brien of Cookham, England, for a number of important suggestions which bore directly on the shape of the work while being drafted. Thanks are also due to Mr. T.L.K. White of Reading, England, who supplied me with invaluable material pertaining to the English martyrs, and Mrs. E. Tate, for loan of certain works which I was unable to locate elsewhere.

I also wish to express my appreciation to the many religious Communities in North America and Europe who supplied me with material relative to the Saints of their Orders.

Finally, I am most indebted to Mr. J.V. Coyle, M.A., of the Institute of Lay Theology, San Francisco, who undertook the reading of my manuscript and its revision, and suggested a number of important modifications which I incorporated into the final draft.

F. W. J.

Feast of All Saints,

November 1, 1963.

CONTENTS

PROLOGUE

CHRISTIANITY is the profession of the life of Christ. — *St Gregory Nazianzen (d. 395).*

A CHRISTIAN has a union with Jesus Christ more noble, more intimate and more perfect than the members of a human body have with their head. — *St John Eudes (1601-80).*

WE too are Christ because we are His members, because we are His Body, because He is our Head, because the whole Christ is Head and Body. — *St Augustine (354-430).*

BY nature, each one of us is enclosed in his own personality, but supernaturally, we are all one. We are made one body in Christ, because we are nourished by one flesh. As Christ is indivisible, we are all one in Him.

Therefore, He asked His Father *"that they may all be One as We also are One."* — *St Cyril of Alexandria (376-444).*

THE Christian life is the continuation and completion of the life of Christ in us. We should be so many Christs here on earth, continuing His life and His works, labouring and suffering in a holy and divine manner in the spirit of Jesus. — *St John Eudes (1601-80).*

LET us therefore give ourselves to God with a great desire to begin to live thus, and beg Him to destroy in us the life of the world of sin, and to establish His life within us. — *St John Eudes (1601-80).*

I

THE CHRISTIAN DUTY

SANCTIFY yourself and you will sanctify society. —
St Francis of Assisi (1181-1226).

★   ★   ★

*How do we fulfil our duties as Christians in the modern
world? How do we apply the maxims of the Gospel to the
surge of modern life? What are our obligations to society?
To our neighbour? To ourself? And above all, to God?
Where, in an unhallowed world, do we find a halo?*

*These fundamental questions pose themselves to each and
every one of us. And in reply, the Saints tell us that unless
we have a clear understanding of the answers, and moreover, resolve to apply ourselves diligently in the attainment
of these answers, which they freely give, we are in effect
walking backwards upon the road that leads to Life.*

YOU must be holy in the way that God asks you to be
holy. God does not ask you to be a Trappist monk or a
hermit. He wills that you sanctify the world and your
everyday life. — *St Vincent Pallotti (1795-1850).*

To be perfect in our vocation is nothing else than to
fulfil the duties which our state of life obliges us to perform, and to accomplish them well, and only for the
honour and love of God. — *St Francis de Sales (1567-
1622).*

LIFE well employed consists in a faithful correspondence
to grace and a good use of the talents given.

2

There is no other religion than this, and the rule of life is the same for all. — *Blessed Théophane Vénard (1829-61)*.

THIS is the business of our life. By labour and prayer, to advance in the grace of God, till we come to that height of perfection in which, with clean hearts, we may behold God. — *St Augustine (354-430)*.

ALL of us can attain to Christian virtue and holiness, no matter in what condition of life we live and no matter what our life-work may be. — *St Francis de Sales (1567-1622)*.

ONE can become a Saint by cultivating literature, in the scientific academies, in the professorial chairs, in the circles of the erudite, no less than amongst the sinners of the world. — *St Vincent Pallotti (1795-1850)*.

YOU will become a Saint by complying exactly with your daily duties. — *St Mary Joseph Rossello (1811-80)*.

* * *

We must try to begin every day with a new ardour.

IF we wish to make any progress in the service of God we must begin every day of our life with new ardour. We must keep ourselves in the presence of God as much as possible and have no other view or end in all our actions but the divine honour. — *St Charles Borromeo (1538-84)*.

CONSIDER every day that you are then for the first time— as it were—beginning; and always act with the same fervour as on the first day you began. — *St Anthony of Padua (1195-1231)*.

OUR actions have a tongue of their own; they have an eloquence of their own, even when the tongue is silent. For deeds prove the lover more than words. — *St Cyril of Jerusalem (315-86)*.

I WILL suggest a means whereby you can praise God all day long, if you wish. Whatever you do, do it well, and you have praised God. — *St Augustine (354-430)*.

THE Lord measures our perfection neither by the multitude nor the magnitude of our deeds, but by the manner in which we perform them. — *St John of the Cross (1542-91)*.

IT is not the actual physical exertion that counts towards a man's progress, nor the nature of the task, but the spirit of faith with which it is undertaken. — *St Francis Xavier (1506-52)*.

GOD bestows more consideration on the purity of intention with which our actions are performed than on the actions themselves. — *St Augustine (354-430)*.

AN action of small value performed with much love of God is far more excellent than one of a higher virtue, done with less love of God. — *St Francis de Sales (1567-1622)*.

REMEMBER that nothing is small in the eyes of God. Do all that you do with love. — *St Thérèse of Lisieux (1873-97)*.

HE does much in the sight of God who does his best, be it ever so little. — *St Peter of Alcantara (1499-1562)*.

GOD asks little, but He gives much. — *St John Chrysostom (347-407)*.

I AM not capable of doing big things, but I want to do everything, even the smallest things, for the greater glory of God. — *St Dominic Savio (1842-57)*.

* * *

Every moment comes to us pregnant with a command from God, only to pass on and plunge into eternity, there to remain forever what we have made it. — *St Francis de Sales (1567-1622)*.

AT this very moment I may, if I desire, become the friend of God. — *St Augustine (354-430)*.

GOD does not ask of us the perfection of tomorrow, nor even of tonight, but only of the present moment. — *St Madeleine Sophie Barat (1779-1865)*.

* * *

We must bear in mind that the Christian life is, above all, a life of action. We were born to labour, not to daydream.

REMEMBER that the Christian life is one of action; not of speech and daydreams. Let there be few words and many deeds, and let them be done well. — *St Vincent Pallotti (1795-1850)*.

ALL devotion which leads to sloth is false. We must love work. — *St Zita (d. 1278)*.

YOUR heart to God and your hands to work. — *St Mary Joseph Rossello (1811-80)*.

LABOUR without stopping; do all the good works you can while you still have the time. — *St John of God (1495-1550)*.

HUMAN nature grows tired of always doing the same thing, and it is God's will that this should be so because of the opportunity of practising two great virtues. The first is perseverance, which will bring us to our goal. The other is steadfastness, which overcomes the difficulties on the way. — *St Vincent de Paul (1580-1660)*.

OUR business is to love what God would have done. He wills our vocation as it is. Let us love that and not trifle away our time hankering after other people's vocations. — *St Francis de Sales (1567-1622)*.

NOTHING seems tiresome or painful when you are working for a Master who pays well; who rewards even a cup of cold water given for love of Him. — *St Dominic Savio (1842-57)*.

It was this thought that led another young Saint to write of the joy found in the midst of wearying monotony.

I FIND a heaven in the midst of saucepans and brooms. — *St Stanislaus Kostka (1550-68)*.

* * *

We should remember that a cheerful disposition goes a long way towards making the burdens of life bearable.

CHEERFULNESS strengthens the heart and makes us persevere in a good life. Therefore the servant of God ought always to be in good spirits. — *St Philip Neri (1515-95)*.

A CHEERFUL and glad spirit attains to perfection much more readily than a melancholy spirit. — *St Philip Neri (1515-95)*.

DURING the course of the day, recollect as often as you can that you stand in the presence of God. Consider what He does and what you are doing. You will find His eyes turned towards you and perpetually fixed on you with an incomparable love. — *St Francis de Sales (1567-1622)*.

WE need no wings to go in search of Him, but have only to find a place where we can be alone and look upon Him present within us. — *St Teresa of Avila (1515-82)*.

* * *

Perhaps there is nothing quite so important in the daily life of a Christian as the need to shine before men with the light of good example.
We should live and act as other Christs, repeatedly setting before the eyes of our fellow men the silent testimony of our deeds and our devotion.

GOOD example is the most efficacious apostolate. You must be as lighted lanterns and shine like brilliant chandeliers among men. By your good example and your words, animate others to know and love God. — *St Mary Joseph Rossello (1811-80)*.

OUR life should be woven through and through with faith and generosity. — *Blessed Raphaela Mary (1850-1925)*.

YOU must practise first, all that you desire to teach others. — *St Bernardine of Siena (1380-1444)*.

THINK well.
Speak well.
Do well.
These three things, through the mercy of God, will make a man go to Heaven. — *St Camillus de Lellis (1550-1614)*.

PRAYER

O FATHER, most merciful, who, in the beginning, didst create us; who, by the Passion of Thine Only Begotten Son, created us anew: work in us now, we beseech Thee, both to will and to do of Thy good pleasure.

Grant us Thy heavenly benediction, that in whatever work we undertake, we may do all to Thy honour and Thy glory, that being kept from sin, and daily increasing in good works, we may show forth some service to Thee. Through Him who, with Thee and the Holy Ghost, liveth and reigneth, God, forever. Amen. — *St Anselm (1033-1109)*.

2

NO MAN CAN SERVE
TWO MASTERS

You either belong wholly to the world or wholly to God. — *St John Vianney (1786-1859)*.

* * *

God has left us the choice of deciding which of the two masters in life we wish to serve.

On one hand is Christ, beckoning us to come to Him that we may have life, and have it more abundantly.

To see what is on the other hand, we must turn our backs to Him...

You cannot please both God and the world at the same time. They are utterly opposed to each other in their thoughts, their desires, and their actions. — *St John Vianney (1786-1859)*.

This world and that to come are two enemies. We cannot therefore be friends to both; but we must resolve which we would forsake and which we would enjoy. — *St Clement (d. 99)*.

* * *

This does not set material goods in opposition to God.
The Saints have drawn a clear distinction between the correct and the incorrect use of material possessions.

9

HE is rich in spirit who has riches in his spirit, or his spirit in riches. He is poor in spirit who has neither riches in his spirit, nor his spirit in riches. — *St Francis de Sales (1567-1622).*

THERE is a vast difference between having poison and being poisoned. Doctors have all kinds of poisons for their use, but they are not poisoned.

In like manner, you may possess riches without being poisoned by them, provided you have them for use, and not by love in your heart. — *St Francis de Sales (1567-1622).*

IT is not a sin to possess riches; but it is sinful to set our heart upon them, to seek them with eagerness, to place our happiness in them, or to employ unlawful means to acquire them. — *St John Baptist de la Salle (1651-1719).*

RICHES are not forbidden, but the pride of them is. — *St John Chrysostom (347-407).*

IN prosperity, give thanks to God with humility and fear lest by pride you abuse God's benefits and so offend Him. — *St Louis, King (1214-70).*

On the other hand...

WHATEVER a man prefers to God, that he makes a god to himself. — *St Cyprian (200-58).*

WHAT a person desires, if he worships it, is to him a god. A vice in the heart is an idol on the altar. — *St Jerome (342-420).*

THE love of worldly possessions is a sort of bird-lime, which entangles the soul, and prevents it flying to God. — *St Augustine (354-430).*

THERE is nothing more wicked than to love money. — *St Anthony of Padua (1195-1231).*

EARTHLY riches are like the reed. Its roots are sunk in the swamp, and its exterior is fair to behold; but inside it is hollow. If a man leans on such a reed, it will snap off and pierce his soul, and his soul will be carried off to hell. — *St Anthony of Padua (1195-1231).*

OF what use are riches in eternity? — *St Aloysius Gonzaga (1568-91).*

THOSE who love money and fickle honours, fall down before the devil and adore him. — *St Anthony of Padua (1195-1231).*

UNHAPPY is the soul enslaved by the love of anything that is mortal. — *St Augustine (354-430).*

NOTHING can satisfy one whom God does not satisfy. — *St Alphonsus Liguori (1696-1787).*

WHO except God can give you peace? Has the world ever been able to satisfy the heart? — *St Gerard Majella (1726-55).*

HOW foolish are they who take the greatest care of the least things, and the least care of the greatest things. — *St Bernard (1090-1153).*

* * *

We have less to suffer in following Christ and His Cross, in treading the strait path, in constant self-denial, than in following the pleasures of the world.

I TELL you that you have less to suffer in following the Cross than in serving the world and its pleasures. — *St John Vianney (1786-1859).*

THOSE who follow the maxims of the world experience nothing but misery, and the flattering expection of happiness is delusive and vain. — *St Augustine (354-430).*

NIGHT follows day; winter, summer; and in this life or the other, sorrows and sufferings follow vanity and sensuality. — *St Maximus the Confessor (540-622).*

We should consider the shortness of time and the length of eternity.

CONSIDER the shortness of time, the length of eternity, and reflect how everything here below comes to an end and passes by. Of what use is it to lean upon that which cannot give support? — *St Gerard Majella (1726-55).*

THE joy of this life is nothing: the joy of after life is everlasting. — *Blessed William Hart (d. 1583).*

THOSE who give themselves up in considerable measure to the consolations of the world do not deserve those of the Holy Spirit. — *St Bernard (1090-1153).*

IT is far easier to convert to God the sensual than the covetous. — *St Philip Neri (1515-1595).*

IF people would do for God what they do for the world, what a great number of Christians would go to Heaven. — *St John Vianney (1786-1859).*

LET us not esteem worldly prosperity or adversity as things real or of any moment, but let us live elsewhere, and raise all our attention to Heaven; esteeming sin as the only true evil, and nothing truly good, but virtue which unites us to God. — *St Gregory Nazianzen (d. 395)*.

WHEN we hear people talk of riches, honours and amusements of the world, let us remember that all things have an end, and let us then say: *"My God, I wish for Thee alone and nothing more."* — *St Alphonsus Liguori (1696-1787)*.

* * *

YOUR life consists in drawing nearer to God. To do this, you must endeavour to detach yourself from visible things and remember that in a short time they will be taken from you. — *Blessed John of Avila (1500-69)*.

WITHDRAW your heart from the world before God takes your body from it. — *Blessed John of Avila (1500-69)*.

LET us detach ourselves in spirit from all that we see and cling to that which we believe. This is the cross which we must imprint on all our daily actions and behaviour. — *St Peter Damian (1007-72)*.

WE must be detached from ourselves because all our being and all our happiness depends, not on us, but on God, according to the words of our Lord: *"He that loveth his life shall lose it"* (*John* 12 : 25), and *"He that hateth his life shall keep it unto life eternal"* (*Ibid*). — *St Ignatius Loyola (1491-1556)*.

THE sacrifice the good Lord wants of us is to die to ourselves. — *St Charles of Sezze (1613-70)*.

WE should always be prepared to give up readily, with the sure belief that the change comes by the Will of God. — *St Vincent de Paul (1580-1660)*.

Having withdrawn ourselves in spirit from the love of material things, we begin to experience true peace and find a perfect contentment.

IN detachment, the spirit finds quiet and repose for coveting nothing. Nothing wearies it by elation, and nothing oppresses it by dejection, because it stands in the centre of its own humility. — *St John of the Cross (1542-91)*.

HOLY indifference is of the nature of pure love which directs the will to that which is most perfect and destroys every obstacle. — *St Vincent de Paul (1580-1660)*.

To be removed from things of the senses is to contemplate things of the spirit. — *St John Climacus (d. 649)*.

DETACHMENT is the secret of perseverance. — *St Sebastian Valfré (1629-1710)*.

How sweet has it been to me to be deprived of the delights of a frivolous world!
   What incomparable joy have I felt after a privation once so dreaded. — *St Augustine (354-430)*.

* * *

LET us attach ourselves to God alone, and turn our eyes and our hopes to Him. — *St Madeleine Sophie Barat (1779-1865)*.

WHATEVER you do, think not of yourself, but of God. — *St Vincent Ferrer (1350-1419)*.

I OUGHT to imagine to myself that there are no others in the world but God and myself. — *St Alphonsus Liguori (1696-1787)*.

LIVE in the world as if only God and your soul were alone in it.
   Then your heart will never be made captive by any earthly thing. — *St John of the Cross (1542-91)*.

LET my soul live as if separated from my body. — *St John of the Cross (1542-91)*.

I NO longer desire to live a purely human life. Make this your choice if you yourselves would be chosen. — *St Ignatius of Antioch (d. 107)*.

I AM no longer my own. Whether I live or whether I die, I belong to my Saviour. I have nothing of my own. God is my all, and my whole being is His. — *St Catherine of Genoa (1447-1510)*.

NOTHING is anything more to me; everything is nothing to me, but Jesus: neither things nor persons, neither ideas nor emotions, neither honour nor sufferings. Jesus is for me honour, delight, heart and soul. — *St Bernadette (1844-79)*.

NOT the goods of the world, but God.
Not riches, but God.
Not honours, but God.
Not distinction, but God.
Not dignities, but God.

Not advancement, but God.
God always and in everything.

                    St Vincent Pallotti (1795-1850).

PRAYER

GRANT, O Lord, that my heart may neither desire nor
seek anything but what is necessary for the fulfilment
of Thy Holy Will.

May health or sickness, riches or poverty, honours or
contempt, humiliations, leave my soul in that state of
perfect detachment to which I desire to attain for Thy
greater honour and Thy greater glory. Amen. —
St Ignatius Loyola (1491-1556).

3

THY WILL BE DONE

LET each look to himself and see what God wants of him and attend to this, leaving all else alone. — *Blessed Henry Suso (d. 1365).*

* * *

How can we know the Will of God in our daily lives?

IT is certain that whatever happens takes place by the Divine Will. — *St Alphonsus Liguori (1696-1787).*

I WILL see the hand of God in all that happens to me, attributing nothing to individual people, who are but instruments used by Him in the work of my sanctification. — *Blessed Raphaela Mary (1850-1925).*

IN all the vicissitudes of life such as illnesses, losses, and so on, be ever mindful to bow with resignation to the Will of God, and repose on these words: "*God will have it so; so be it done.*" — *St Alphonsus Liguori (1696-1787).*

MAN'S salvation and perfection consist in doing the Will of God, which he must have in view in all things and at every moment of his life.

The more he accomplishes this Divine Will, the more perfect he will be. — *St Peter Claver (1581-1654).*

Man's eternal salvation, therefore, consists in doing the Will of God in his daily life. This in turn demands a constant striving on the part of the body to suppress all tendencies and desires which run counter to the law of Christ. "Unless you deny yourself," warns our Saviour, "you cannot be my disciple."

IF you do not learn to deny yourself, you can make no progress in perfection. — *St John of the Cross (1542-91).*

NOTHING but self-will can separate us from God. — *St Alphonsus Liguori (1696-1787).*

WHENCE is all disturbance of mind, if not from following one's own desires? — *St Bernard (1090-1153).*

HE who is his own master is a scholar under a fool. — *St Bernard (1090-1153).*

TAKE away self-will, and there will be no Hell. — *St Bernard (1090-1153).*

* * *

THE merit of renouncing one's own will is invariably greater and more precious than getting one's own way. — *Blessed John Ruysbroeck (1293-1381).*

THE more we conquer ourselves the more He gives us of His grace; and if today we have had power to overcome one difficulty, tomorrow and the day after we shall be able to surmount others that are much greater and more distressing. — *St Vincent de Paul (1580-1660).*

TURN yourself round like a piece of clay and say to the Lord: I am clay, and you, Lord, the potter. Make of me what you will. — *Blessed John of Avila (1500-69).*

FEED upon the Will of God and drink the chalice of Jesus with your eyes shut, so that you may not see what is inside. Let it be enough for you to know that it is the cup of your sweet Jesus. — *St Vincent de Paul (1580-1660)*.

YOU will advance in proportion as you deny your own self. — *St Jerome (342-420)*.

* * *

CHRIST does not force our will, He only takes what we give Him. But He does not give Himself entirely until He sees that we yield ourselves entirely to Him. — *St Teresa of Avila (1515-82)*.

FEW souls understand what God would accomplish in them if they were to abandon themselves unreservedly to Him and if they were to allow His grace to mould them accordingly. — *St Ignatius Loyola (1491-1556)*.

BY renouncing one's own will, it is possible to reach the highest perfection. — *Blessed Raphaela Mary (1850-1925)*.

LOVE consumes us only in the measure of our self-surrender. — *St Thérèse of Lisieux (1873-97)*.

HE who wills only what God wills, possesses all that he desires. For whatever happens to him, happens by the Will of God. — *St Alphonsus Liguori (1696-1787)*.

A martyr about to give his life for Christ expressed himself thus:

GOD gave Himself to thee: give thyself to God. — *Blessed Robert Southwell (1561-95)*.

HE gave Himself wholly to you: He left nothing for Himself. — *St John Chrysostom (347-407)*.

The Kingdom of Heaven, O man, requires
No other price than yourself.
The value of it is yourself.
Give yourself for it and you shall have it. — *St Augustine (354-430)*.

By giving yourself to God, you not only receive Himself in exchange, but eternal life as well. — *St Francis de Sales (1567-1622)*.

PRAYER

LORD Jesus, may I know myself and know Thee.
And desire nothing save only Thee.
May I hate myself and love Thee.
May I do everything for the sake of Thee.
May I humble myself and exalt Thee.
May I think of nothing except Thee.
May I die to myself and live in Thee.
May I receive whatever happens as from Thee.
May I banish self and follow Thee
And ever desire to follow Thee.
May I fly from myself and fly to Thee,
That I may deserve to be defended by Thee.
May I fear for myself and fear Thee.
And be among those who are chosen by Thee.
May I distrust myself and trust in Thee.
May I be willing to obey on account of Thee.
May I cling to nothing but to Thee.
May I be poor for the sake of Thee.
    Look upon me that I may love Thee.
    Call me that I may see Thee,
    And ever and ever enjoy Thee. Amen. — *St Augustine (354-430)*.

4

THE GREATEST COMMANDMENT

To love God is something greater than to know Him.
—*St Thomas Aquinas (1225-74)*.

* * *

CHARITY may be a very short word, but with its tremendous meaning of pure love, it sums up man's entire relation to God and to his neighbour. As our Lord explained: *"It is on charity that all the Law and the prophets depend."* — *St Aelred of Rievaulx (1110-67)*.

ALL is contained in these brief words: *"Love the Lord thy God with all thy heart, and with thy soul, and with all thy strength: and love thy neighbour as thyself."* — *St Augustine (354-430)*.

MAN is the perfection of the Universe.
The spirit is the perfection of man.
Love is the perfection of the spirit, and charity that of love.
Therefore, the love of God is the end, the perfection of the Universe. — *St Francis de Sales (1567-1622)*.

YOU ask me for a method of attaining perfection.
I know of love—and only love.
Love can do all things. — *St Thérèse of Lisieux (1873-97)*.

PERFECTION of life is the perfection of love. For love is the life of the soul. — *St Francis de Sales (1567-1622)*.

* * *

WE should love God because He is God, and the measure of our love should be to love Him without measure. — *St Bernard (1090-1153)*.

NOT without reward is God loved, although He should be loved without thought of reward. — *St Bernard (1090-1153)*.

IN the royal galley of Divine Love, there is no galley slave: all the rowers are volunteers. — *St Francis de Sales (1567-1622)*.

WE are not drawn to God by iron chains, but by sweet attractions and holy inspirations. — *St Francis de Sales (1567-1622)*.

WE must fear God out of love, not love Him out of fear. — *St Francis de Sales (1567-1622)*.

To love God as He ought to be loved, we must be detached from all temporal love. We must love nothing but Him, or if we love anything else, we must love it only for His sake. — *St Peter Claver (1581-1654)*.

IF we love God above all things, then the little streams of our lawful affections will lose themselves in the Divine wellspring. — *St Madeleine Sophie Barat (1779-1865)*.

GOD must be loved first, in order that one's neighbour, too, may be loved in God. — *St Bernard (1090-1153)*.

* * *

The depth of our love of God must be measured by the desire we have to suffer for His sake.

HE who wishes to love God does not truly love Him if he has not an ardent and constant desire to suffer for His sake. — *St Aloysius Gonzaga (1568-91)*.

WHAT a weakness it is to love Jesus Christ only when He caresses us, and to be cold immediately He afflicts us. This is not true love. Those who love thus, love themselves too much to love God with all their heart. — *St Margaret Mary Alacoque (1647-90)*.

I WILL not live an instant that I do not live in love. Whoever loves does all things without suffering, or, suffering, loves his suffering. — *St Augustine (354-430)*.

UNDER the influence of fear, we bear the Cross of Christ with patience. Under the more inspiring influence of hope, we carry the Cross with a firm and valiant heart. But under the consuming power of love, we embrace the Cross with ardour. — *St Bernard (1090-1153)*.

THE heart of Jesus desires to be everything to the heart that It loves. But that will only be by suffering for Him. — *St Margaret Mary Alacoque (1647-90)*.

* * *

Unless we love God, we can scarcely persevere in grace.

HE who does not acquire the love of God will scarcely persevere in the grace of God, for it is very difficult to renounce sin merely through fear of chastisement. — *St Alphonsus Liguori (1696-1787)*.

WHAT does it avail to know that there is a God, which thou not only believest by Faith, but also knowest by reason: what does it avail that thou knowest Him if thou think little of Him? — *St Thomas More (1478-1535)*.

WHAT do you possess if you possess not God? — *St Augustine (354-430)*.

IF the greatest sinner on earth should repent at the moment of death, and draw his last breath in an act of love; neither the many graces he had abused, nor the many sins he had committed would stand in his way. Our Lord would receive him into His mercy. — *St Thérèse of Lisieux (1873-97)*.

* * *

The love of God is the harbinger of enduring peace.

IF we love God and are faithful to Him, we shall be at peace, and this peace will endure. — *St Madeleine Sophie Barat (1779-1865)*.

THE soul who is in love with God is a gentle, humble and patient soul. — *St John of the Cross (1542-91)*.

THE price of Divine Love is not to be appreciated; for it suffices to obtain the Kingdom of Heaven, and the love of Him who has loved us so much merits the highest degree of our love. — *St Francis of Assisi (1181-1226)*.

DAILY advance, then, in this love, both by praying and by well-doing, that through the help of Him who enjoined it on you, and whose gift it is, it may be nourished and increased, until, being perfected, it render you perfect. — *St Augustine (354-430)*.

LOVE God, serve God: everything is in that. — *St Clare of Assisi (1193-1253)*.

PRAYER

O SACRED Heart of Jesus! Living and life-giving Fountain of eternal life, infinite treasure of the Divinity, glowing furnace of Love! Thou art my refuge and my sanctuary.

O my adorable and lovely Saviour, consume my heart with that burning fire with which Thine is inflamed. Pour down on my soul those graces which flow from Thy Love, and let my heart be so united with Thine, that our wills may be one, and mine in all things conformed to Thine. May Thy Will be the rule alike of my desires and of all my actions. Amen. — *St Gertrude (d. 1302).*

5

CHARITY IN ACTION

To love our neighbour in charity is to love God in man. — *St Francis de Sales (1567-1622)*.

★ ★ ★

Charity is the golden link between God and man.

CHARITY is the sweet and holy bond which links the soul with its Creator: it binds God with man and man with God. — *St Catherine of Siena (1347-80)*.

CHARITY is the form, mover, mother and root of all the virtues. — *St Thomas Aquinas (1225-74)*.

CHARITY is that with which no man is lost, and without which no man is saved. — *St Robert Bellarmine (1542-1621)*.

SALVATION is shown to faith, it is prepared for hope, but it is given only to charity.

Faith points out the way to the land of promise as a pillar of fire; hope feeds us with its manna of sweetness, but charity actually introduces us into the Promised Land. — *St Francis de Sales (1567-1622)*.

IT is by the path of love, which is charity, that God draws near to man, and man to God. But where charity is not found, God cannot dwell.

If, then, we possess charity, we possess God, for God is Charity *(1 John 4. 8). — St Albert the Great (d. 1280).*

* * *

Our love of God is manifested by the love we bear towards our neighbour.

HE alone loves the Creator perfectly who manifests a pure love for his neighbour. — *St Bede the Venerable (673-735).*

SINCE God is perfect in loving man, man must be perfect in loving his neighbour. — *St Vincent Pallotti (1795-1850).*

GOD does not command us to live dressed in hair-shirts and chains, or to chastise our flesh with scourges, but to love Him above all things and our neighbour as ourselves. — *St Charles of Sezze (1613-70).*

WE must love our neighbour as being made in the image of God and as an object of His love. — *St Vincent de Paul (1580-1660).*

WE ought to respect the image of God in everyone. It is there. — *Blessed Raphaela Mary (1850-1925).*

I SEE in my neighbour the Person of Jesus Christ. — *St Gerard Majella (1726-55).*

Charity knows no bounds of race, colour, creed or distance. The parable of the Good Samaritan proclaims that everyone is our neighbour. The tiny orphan wandering and wailing through some evil smelling Hong Kong slum, the blind beggar squatting awkwardly on a teeming Bombay sidewalk, unwept and unheeded—or nearer home, the sick, the aged, the unemployed; all need our prayers or alms or both. For charity is the great white dividing line between the children of God and the children of men.

ALL our religion is but a false religion, and all our virtues are mere illusions and we ourselves are only hypocrites in the sight of God, if we have not that universal charity for everyone—for the good, and for the bad, for the poor and for the rich, and for all those who do us harm as much as for those who do us good. — *St John Vianney (1786-1859).*

THE proof of love is in the works.
Where love exists, it works great things.
But when it ceases to act, it ceases to exist. — *St Gregory the Great (d. 604).*

* * *

IT is to those who have the most need of us that we ought to show our love more especially. — *St Francis de Sales (1567-1622).*

IF we are able to enter the church day and night and implore God to hear our prayers, how careful should we be to hear and grant the petitions of our neighbour in need. — *St John the Almoner (d. 619?).*

EXTEND mercy towards others, so that there can be no one in need whom you meet without helping. For what hope is there for us if God should withdraw His Mercy from us? — *St Vincent de Paul (1580-1660).*

THE Church teaches us that mercy belongs to God. Let us implore Him to bestow on us the spirit of mercy and compassion, so that we are filled with it and may never lose it. Only consider how much we ourselves are in need of mercy. — *St Vincent de Paul (1580-1660)*.

WE must show charity towards the sick, who are in greater need of help. Let us take them some small gift if they are poor, or, at least, let us go and wait on them and comfort them. — *St Alphonsus Liguori (1696-1787)*.

THE Most Blessed Sacrament is Christ made visible. The poor sick person is Christ again made visible. *St Gerard Majella (1726-55)*.

WE should strive to keep our hearts open to the sufferings and wretchedness of other people, and pray continually that God may grant us that spirit of compassion which is truly of the Spirit of God. — *St Vincent de Paul (1580-1660)*.

Gazing upon us are the sad eyes of all the hungry children in the world...

LET us relieve the poverty of those that beg of us and let us not be over-exact about it. — *St John Chrysostom (347-407)*.

WE must give alms. Charity wins souls and draws them to virtue. — *St Angela Merici (1474-1540)*.

NOTHING makes us so prosperous in this world as to give alms. — *St Francis de Sales (1567-1622)*.

ALMS are an inheritance and a justice which is due to the poor, and which Jesus Christ has levied upon us. — *St Francis of Assisi (1181-1226)*.

GOD has no need of your money, but the poor have. You give it to the poor, and God receives it. — *St Augustine (354-430).*

THE poor stretch forth the hand, but God receives what is offered. — *St Peter Chrysologus (d. 450).*

IT is God's way to give much for little. Our Lord does not attend to how much we give, but to the generosity of our will, and for this very reason He makes much of a little. — *St John Chrysostom (347-407).*

BELIEVE me, he who does not think of the wants of the poor is not a member of the body of Christ. For if one member suffers, all suffer. — *St Elphege (d. 1012).*

WE must sacrifice everything for the poor. — *St Gerard Majella (1726-55).*

BE diligent in serving the poor. Love the poor. Honour them, as you would Christ Himself. — *St Louise de Marillac (1591-1660).*

LOVE the poor tenderly, regarding them as your masters and yourselves as their servants. — *St John of God (1495-1550).*

GOD loves the poor, and consequently He loves those who have an affection for the poor. For when we love anyone very much, we also love his friends. — *St Vincent de Paul (1580-1660).*

I WANT to be able to say to Jesus: "*Jesus, when you were hungry, I gave you to eat. When you were naked, I clothed you. When you were sick, I visited you.*" — *St Elizabeth of Hungary (1207-31).*

* * *

Turning over the golden coin of Charity, the Saints reveal for us a course of practical guidance in the sphere of human relationships.

IN order to avoid discord, never contradict anyone except in case of sin or some danger to a neighbour; and when necessary to contradict others, do it with tact and not with temper. — *St Louis, King (1214-70).*

YOU should do no harm to anybody whatsoever, and as much as it is possible, do good to all. — *St Peter Fourier (1565-1640).*

TOLERANCE is an important part of charity. Without it, it is difficult for two persons to get on together. Moreover, tolerance is the bond of all friendship, and unites people in heart and opinion and action, not only with each other, but in unity with our Lord, so that they may really be at peace. — *St Vincent de Paul (1580-1660).*

NEVER utter in your neighbours' absence what you would not say in their presence. — *St Mary Magdalen of Pazzi (1566-1607).*

IF we wish to keep peace with our neighbour, we should never remind any one of his natural defects. — *St Philip Neri (1515-95).*

WOULD we wish that our own hidden sins should be divulged?
    We ought, then, to be silent regarding those of others. *"Hast thou heard a word against thy neighbour? Let it die within thee, trusting that it will not burst thee."* (Ecclus. xix. 10). — *St John Baptist de la Salle (1651-1719).*

WE must desire our neighbour's good and rejoice when he obtains it. And on the other hand, we must be sorry for his misfortunes. — *St Alphonsus Liguori (1696-1787).*

WE must neither judge nor suspect evil of our neighbour, without good grounds. — *St Alphonsus Liguori (1696-1787).*

WHEN it seems that God shows us the faults of others, keep on the safer side. It may be that thy judgment is false. — *St Catherine of Siena (1347-80).*

Do not condemn, even with your eyes, for they are often deceived. — *St John Climacus (d. 649).*

IN our neighbour, we should observe only what is good. — *St Jeanne de Chantal (1572-1641).*

LET us be careful not to repeat to anyone the evil that has been said of him by another. For the Scripture warns that he who sows discord is hated by God. — *St Alphonsus Liguori (1696-1787).*

WE must abstain from the least shadow of detraction. A detractor is hateful to God and man. — *St Alphonsus Liguori (1696-1787).*

DETRACTION, like fire borne onwards by the wind, passes from mouth to mouth, and what it does not destroy, it blackens. — *St John Baptist de la Salle (1651-1719).*

YOU will effect more by kind words and a courteous manner, than by anger or sharp rebuke, which should never be used but in necessity. — *St Angela Merici (1474-1540).*

IF anyone blames or accuses me, I will strive to make all bitter feelings pass gently away. — *St Gerard Majella (1726-55)*.

* * *

True charity is the ultimate Christian goal.

TRUE charity consists in putting up with all one's neighbour's faults, never being surprised by his weakness, and being inspired by the least of his virtues. — *St Thérèse of Lisieux (1873-97)*.

TRUE charity consists in doing good to those who do us evil, and in thus winning them over. — *St Alphonsus Liguori (1696-1787)*.

TRUE charity means returning good for evil—always. — *St Mary Mazzarello (1837-81)*.

WE must always choose the most perfect. Two good works present themselves to be done, one in favour of a person we love, the other in favour of a person who has done us some harm. Well, we must give preference to the latter. — *St John Vianney (1786-1859)*.

WE must above all show charity to our enemies. "*Do good to those that hate you*" (*Matt. v. 44*). By this you may know that a man is a true Christian, if he seeks to do good to those who wish him evil. — *St Alphonsus Liguori (1696-1787)*.

LET us also pray for those who persecute us—this is the way the Saints revenged themselves.

He who pardons anyone who has offended him is sure of being pardoned by God, since God has given us the promise: "*Forgive, and you shall be forgiven.*" — *St Alphonsus Liguori (1696-1787)*.

To harbour no envy, no anger, no resentment against an offender is still not to have charity for him. It is possible, without any charity, to avoid rendering evil for evil. But to render, spontaneously, good for evil—such belongs to a perfect spiritual love. — *St Maximus the Confessor (d. 622)*.

LET us also remember to be charitable to our neighbours who are dead. We should endeavour to help them, either by having Masses said for them, or by hearing Masses for them, by giving alms, or at least by praying and applying indulgences in their behalf. — *St Alphonsus Liguori (1696-1787)*.

AT the end of our life, we shall all be judged by charity. — *St John of the Cross (1542-91)*.

PRAYER

LORD, make me an instrument of Thy peace!
Where there is hatred, let me sow love.
Where there is injury, pardon.
Where there is doubt, faith.
Where there is despair, hope.
Where there is darkness, light.
Where there is sadness, joy.

O Divine Master! Grant that I may
Not so much seek
To be consoled, as to console;
To be understood, as to understand;
To be loved, as to love.

For

It is in giving that we receive.
It is in pardoning that we are pardoned.
It is in dying that we are born to Eternal Life. — *St Francis of Assisi (1181-1226)*.

6

THE POWER OF PRAYER

THE power of prayer is really tremendous. —
St Thérèse of Lisieux (1873-97).

* * *

*Prayer is the noblest utterance of man, the very breath
of the soul.*
It is as necessary as life itself.

THE air which we breathe, the bread which we eat, the
heart which throbs in our bosoms, are not more necessary for man that he may live as a human being, than
is prayer for the Christian that he may live as a Christian.
— *St John Eudes (1601-80).*

As our body cannot live without nourishment, so our
soul cannot spiritually be kept alive without prayer. —
St Augustine (354-430).

PRAYER is necessary for salvation; and therefore God,
who desires that we should be saved, has enjoined it as
a precept. — *St Alphonsus Liguori (1696-1787).*

IF we would be saved and become Saints, we ought
always to stand at the gates of the Divine mercy to beg
and pray for, as an alms, all that we need. — *St Alphonsus Liguori (1696-1787).*

IT is simply impossible to lead, without the aid of prayer,
a virtuous life. — *St John Chrysostom (347-407).*

The Saints have left us a perfect example of prayer.

THE whole lives of the Saints have been one of meditation and prayer. All the graces by means of which they have become Saints were received by them in answer to their prayers. — *St Alphonsus Liguori (1696-1787).*

They have sung of the beauty and the power of prayer with the language of poetry.
Prayer is...

A MANIFESTATION of Divine glory. — *St John of Damascus (690 -749).*

A TREASURE. — *St Alphonsus Liguori (1696-1787).*

THE key to Heaven. — *St Augustine (354-430).*

MAN'S greatest virtue. — *St Peter Julian Eymard (1811-68).*

A PIOUS way of forcing God. — *St John Climacus (d. 649).*

THE bridge over temptations, and the death of sadness and the token of future glory. — *St John Climacus (d. 649).*

THE holy water that by its flow makes the plants of our good desires grow green and flourish. — *St Francis de Sales (1567-1622).*

A WINE which makes glad the heart of man. — *St Bernard (1090-1153).*

AN importunity which becomes our opportunity. — *St Jerome (342-420).*

AN uplifting of the heart; a cry of gratitude and love. — *St Thérèse of Lisieux (1873-97)*.

* * *

WE must pray without ceasing, in every occurrence and employment of our lives—that prayer which is rather a habit of lifting up the heart to God as in a constant communication with Him. — *Blessed Elizabeth Seton (1774-1821)*.

WE must pray without tiring, for the salvation of mankind does not depend on material success; nor on sciences that cloud the intellect. Neither does it depend on arms and human industries, but on Jesus alone. — *St Frances Xavier Cabrini (1850-1917)*.

The more we pray, the more we receive.

HE who prays most receives most. — *St Alphonsus Liguori (1696-1787)*.

VIRTUES are formed by prayer.
Prayer preserves temperance.
Prayer suppresses anger.
Prayer prevents emotions of pride and envy.
Prayer draws into the soul the Holy Ghost,
And raises man to Heaven. — *St Ephraem (306-73)*.

WHEN prayer is poured forth, sins are covered. — *St Ambrose (340-97)*.

FAITH believes, hope prays, and charity begs in order to give to others. Humility of heart forms the prayer, confidence speaks it, and perseverance triumphs over God Himself. — *St Peter Julian Eymard (1811-68)*.

By prayer, man gives God the greatest glory possible. — *St Peter Julian Eymard (1811-68)*.

PRAYER ascends and mercy descends. High as are the heavens and low as is the earth, God hears the voice of man. — *St Augustine (354-430)*.

DILIGENCE in prayer is the perfection of the Gospel. — *St Aloysius Gonzaga (1568-91)*.

PRAYER brings about the perfect absorption of the food of our good actions, and distributes them into all the members of the soul. — *St Bernard (1090-1153)*.

WHAT does it cost us to say: *"My God, help me! Have mercy on me!"* Is there anything easier than this? And this little will suffice to save us if we be diligent in doing it. — *St Alphonsus Liguori (1696-1787)*.

* * *

The Saints counsel us to pray with humility and confidence, and never cease to persevere.

THE prayer of a humble soul penetrates the heavens and presents itself before the throne of God and does not leave without God's looking on it and hearing it. *"The prayer of him that humbleth himself shall pierce the clouds, ... and he will not depart till the Most High behold."* *(Ecclus. 35:21)*. — *St Alphonsus Liguori (1696-1787)*.

IT is on humble souls that God pours down His fullest light and grace. He teaches them what scholars cannot learn, and mysteries that the wisest cannot solve He can make plain to them. — *St Vincent de Paul (1580-1660)*.

OUR Lord gives to souls of prayer a deep understanding of Himself. He never deceives them. — *St Peter Julian Eymard (1811-68)*.

PRAYER reveals to souls the vanity of earthly goods and pleasures. It fills them with light, strength and consolation; and gives them a foretaste of the calm bliss of our heavenly home. — *St Rose of Viterbo (d. 1252)*.

* * *

PRAY with great confidence, with confidence based upon the goodness and infinite generosity of God and upon the promises of Jesus Christ. God is a spring of living water which flows unceasingly into the hearts of those who pray. — *St Louis de Montfort (1673-1716)*.

PRAYER is to our soul what rain is to the soil. Fertilize the soil ever so richly, it will remain barren unless fed by frequent rains. — *St John Vianney (1786-1859)*.

WE should have frequent recourse to prayer, and persevere a long time in it. God wishes to be solicited. He is not weary of hearing us. The treasure of His graces is infinite. We can do nothing more pleasing to Him than to beg incessantly that He bestow them upon us. — *St John Baptist de la Salle (1651-1719)*.

IT is essential to begin the practice of prayer with a firm resolution of persevering in it. — *St Teresa of Avila (1515-82)*.

BY humble and faithful prayer, the soul acquires, with time and perseverance, every virtue. — *St Catherine of Siena (1347-80)*.

SPIRITUAL joy arises from purity of the heart and perseverance in prayer. — *St Francis of Assisi (1181-1226).*

ONLY he will receive, will find, and will enter who perseveres in asking, seeking and knocking. — *St Louis de Montfort (1673-1716).*

THE more we pray, the more we wish to pray. Like a fish which at first swims on the surface of the water, and afterwards plunges down, and is always going deeper; the soul plunges, dives, and loses itself in the sweetness of conversing with God. — *St John Vianney (1786-1859).*

HE who does not give up prayer cannot possibly continue to offend God habitually. Either he will give up prayer, or he will stop sinning. — *St Alphonsus Liguori (1696-1787).*

* * *

The Saints give us practical guidance as to how we should pray.

WHEN you have asked the Holy Spirit to help you pray well, put yourself for a moment in the presence of God. — *St Louis de Montfort (1673-1716).*

BEFORE prayer, endeavour to realize whose Presence you are approaching, and to whom you are about to speak. We can never fully understand how we ought to behave towards God, before whom the angels tremble. — *St Teresa of Avila (1515-82).*

THE great method of prayer is to have none. If in going to prayer one can form in oneself a pure capacity for receiving the spirit of God, that will suffice for all method. — *St Jeanne de Chantal (1572-1641)*.

STRETCH forth your hand towards God as an infant towards its father to be conducted by Him. — *St Francis de Sales (1567-1622)*.

PRAYER ought to be short and pure, unless it be prolonged by the inspiration of Divine grace. — *St Benedict (480-547)*.

LET us ask our Lord to work in us and through us, and let us do our utmost to draw Him down into our hearts, for He Himself has said: "*Without Me you can do nothing.*" — *St Madeleine Sophie Barat (1779-1865)*.

PRAYER should be accomplished by grace and not by artifice. — *St Jeanne de Chantal (1572-1641)*.

GOD, the Creator of all things, is so full of mercy and compassion that whatever may be the grace for which we stretch out our hands, we shall not fail to receive it. — *St Bernard (1090-1153)*.

GOD is more anxious to bestow His blessings on us than we are to receive them. — *St Augustine (354-430)*.

GOD wishes to be asked, He wishes to be forced, He wishes, in a certain manner, to be overcome by our prayer. — *St Gregory the Great (d. 604)*.

HE would not urge us to ask, unless He were willing to give. — *St Augustine (354-430)*.

FOR prayer to be effective, our petitions should be for benefits worthily to be expected from God. "*Ye ask, and receive not because ye ask amiss"* (*James 4. 3*). — St Thomas Aquinas (1225-74).

GOD will not hear our prayers unless we acknowledge ourselves to be sinners. We do this when we ponder on our own sins alone, and not on those of our neighbour. — *St Moses the Ethiopian (IVth century).*

HE knows how to live well who knows how to pray well. — *St Augustine (354-430).*

IT is not so much the length of a prayer, but the fervour with which it is said which pleases Almighty God and touches His Heart. — *St Louis de Montfort (1673-1716).*

WHEN we pray, the voice of the heart must be heard more than that proceeding from the mouth. — *St Bonaventure (1221-74).*

IT is better to say one Pater Noster fervently and devoutly than a thousand with no devotion and full of distraction. — *St Edmund (841-70).*

* * *

Why are our prayers not always answered?

HE who faithfully prays to God for the necessaries of this life is both mercifully heard, and mercifully not heard. For the physician knows better than the sick man what is good for the disease.—*St Augustine (354-430).*

WE ought to be persuaded that what God refuses to our prayer, He grants to our salvation. — *St Augustine (354-430).*

THE reason why sometimes thou hast asked and not received, is because thou hast asked amiss, either inconsistently, or lightly, or because thou hast asked for what was not good for thee, or because thou hast ceased asking. — *St Basil (329-79)*.

* * *

NEVER address your words to God while you are thinking of something else. — *St Teresa of Avila (1515-82)*.

ONE whose soul is in disorder, whose mind is wandering with vain, useless thoughts, cannot pray. To pray, we must unite the flesh and its feelings to the soul with its imagination, memory and will. — *St Frances Xavier Cabrini (1850-1917)*.

PURPOSELY to allow one's mind to wander in prayer is sinful and hinders the prayer from having fruit. — *St Thomas Aquinas (1225-74)*.

HE who fights even the smallest distractions faithfully when he says even the very smallest prayer, will also be faithful in great things. — *St Louis de Montfort (1673-1716)*.

I HAVE many distractions, but as soon as I am aware of them, I pray for those people the thought of whom is diverting my attention. In this way, they reap the benefit of my distractions. — *St Thérèse of Lisieux (1873-97)*.

WHEN I am incapable of praying, I want to keep telling Him that I love Him. It's not difficult, and it keeps the *fire* going. — *St Thérèse of Lisieux (1873-97)*.

* * *

To offer prayers for the conversion of sinners is one of the surest ways of proving our love for God.

If we love God as we should, with all our heart, soul, mind and strength, we naturally desire all to believe, adore, hope and love Him. Sin, wherever it is committed, evokes our common sorrow. Reparation and prayer for the sinner arise spontaneously in our hearts.

WE should pray hard for the conversion of sinners. In Heaven, there is more joy over the conversion of one sinner than over many just who are saved. — *Blessed Raphaela Mary (1850-1925).*

To pray for those who are in mortal sin is the best kind of almsgiving. For the love of God, always remember such souls when you pray. — *St Teresa of Avila (1515-82).*

THE devil strains every nerve to secure the souls which belong to Christ. We should not grudge our toil in wresting them from Satan, and giving them back to God. — *St Sebastian (d. 288).*

HE causes his prayers to be of more avail to himself, who offers them also for others. — *St Gregory the Great (d. 604).*

* * *

The greatest of all prayers and the one most recommended to us is the Rosary...

THE Holy Rosary is the storehouse of countless blessings. — *Blessed Alan de la Roche (1428-75).*

NEVER will anyone who says his Rosary every day be led astray.

This is a statement that I would gladly sign with my blood. — *St Louis de Montfort (1673-1716).*

IF you say the Rosary faithfully unto death, I do assure you that, in spite of the gravity of your sins, *"you will receive a never fading crown of glory"* (1 Peter 5. 4). — *St Louis de Montfort (1673-1716).*

WHEN the Holy Rosary is said well, it gives Jesus and Mary more glory and is more meritorious than any other prayer. — *St Louis de Montfort (1673-1716).*

RECITE your Rosary with faith, with humility, with confidence and with perseverance. — *St Louis de Montfort (1673-1716).*

BEFORE beginning a decade, pause for a moment or two and contemplate the mystery that you are about to honour in that decade. — *St Louis de Montfort (1673-1716).*

WHAT prayer could be more true before God the Father than that which the Son, who is Truth, uttered with His own lips? — *St John Chrysostom (347-407).*

IF you are to recite the Our Father well, one thing is necessary: you must not leave the side of the Master who has taught it to you. — *St Teresa of Avila (1515-82).*

WHENEVER we say the Our Father devoutly, our venial sins are forgiven. — *St Augustine (354-430).*

THE Our Father contains all the duties we owe to God, the acts of all the virtues and the petitions for all our spiritual and corporal needs. — *St Louis de Montfort (1673-1716)*.

THE Angelic Salutation is a rainbow in the heavens, a sign of the mercy and grace which God has given to the world. — *Blessed Alan de la Roche (1428-75)*.

WHEN our hands have touched spices, they give fragrance to all they handle. Let us make our prayers pass through the hands of the Blessed Virgin. She will make them fragrant. — *St John Vianney (1786-1859)*.

PRAYER

ETERNAL Father, Thy Son has promised that Thou wilt grant us all the graces that we shall ask of Thee in His name. Trusting, then, in this great promise, I, in the name and through the merits of Jesus Christ, ask of Thee the following graces:

First, I ask the pardon of all the offences I have committed, for which I am sorry above all things with my whole heart, because I have offended Thy infinite goodness.

Secondly, I ask Thy Divine light, which will make me see the vanity of all the goods of this earth, and Thy infinite greatness and goodness.

Thirdly, I ask Thy holy love, which will detach me from all creatures, and particularly from myself, that I may love nothing but Thee, and Thy most holy will.

Fourthly, give me confidence in the merits of Jesus Christ and in the patronage of Mary.

Fifthly, I ask holy perseverance in Thy grace. I resolve in all my temptations and necessities, to have recourse to Thee; and I am certain that as often as I recommend myself to Thee, I shall receive Thy aid; but I fear that I shall neglect to have recourse to Thee, and that this neglect may be the cause of my ruin.

Ah! Eternal Father, through the love which Thou dost bear to Jesus Christ, grant me the grace of prayer, the grace to pray always to Thee for Thine aid, always repeating, *My God, assist me, my Jesus, mercy; Mary, my Mother, pray for me. Amen.* — *St Alphonsus Liguori (1696-1787).*

7

HUMILITY

THERE is more value in a little study of humility and in a single act of it than in all the knowledge in the world. — *St Teresa of Avila (1515-82)*.

* * *

THE gate of Heaven is very low; only the humble can enter it. — *Blessed Elizabeth Seton (1774-1821)*.

No man can attain to the knowledge of God but by humility. The way to mount high is to descend. — *Blessed Giles of Assisi (d. 1262)*.

YOU aspire to great things? Begin with little ones. You desire to erect a very high building? Think first of the foundation of humility. The higher one intends it, the deeper must the foundations be laid. — *St Augustine (354-430)*.

What is humility?

HUMILITY has been regarded by the Saints as the basis and guardian of all virtues. — *St Alphonsus Liguori (1696-1787)*.

It is...

THE mother of salvation. — *St Bernard (1090-1153)*.

THE foundation of sanctity. — *St Cyprian (200-58)*.

THE key which opens all the treasures of God. — *St Mary Euphrasia Pelletier (1796-1868)*.

THE only virtue no devil can imitate. If pride made demons out of angels, there is no doubt that humility could make angels out of demons. — *St John Climacus (d. 649)*.

HUMILITY is so precious that it obtains the things that are too high to be taught. It attains and possesses what words do not attain. — *Blessed John Ruysbroeck (1293-1381)*.

Even the possession of every virtue is of no avail if we have not acquired humility.

IF we possessed every virtue, but lacked humility, those virtues would be without root and would not last. — *St Vincent de Paul (1580-1660)*.

* * *

How can we achieve this supreme virtue in our daily lives?

IN truth, the soul can possess no better insight for knowledge than to perceive its own nothingness. — *St Angela of Foligno (d. 1312)*.

BELIEVE that others are better than you in the depths of their souls, although outwardly you may appear better than they. — *St Augustine (354-430)*.

WE must never glance at what is good in ourselves, much less ponder over it, but we should search out what is wrong and what is lacking. This is an excellent way of remaining humble. — *St Vincent de Paul (1580-1660)*.

WE often say that we are nothing. But we would be very sorry if anyone should take us at our word. We pretend to retire and hide ourselves, so that the world may run after us and seek us out. True humility does not make a show of herself or use many humble words; for she desires not only to conceal all other virtues, but most of all to conceal herself. — *St Francis de Sales (1567-1622).*

THAT man is truly humble who converts humiliation into humility. — *St Bernard (1090-1153).*

HOWEVER great the work that God may achieve by an individual, he must not indulge in self-satisfaction. He ought rather to be all the more humbled, seeing himself merely as a tool which God has made use of. — *St Vincent de Paul (1580-1660).*

To remain humble, we should often reflect on the greatness and humiliations of the Blessed Virgin. — *Blessed Margaret Bourgeoys (1620-1700).*

CERTAINLY nothing can so effectually humble us before the mercy of God as the multitude of His benefits. Nor can anything so much humble us before His justice as the enormity of our innumerable offences. Let us consider what He has done for us and what we have done against Him. — *St Francis de Sales (1567-1622).*

REMEMBER that Jesus Christ, referring to the humility of the publican, said that his prayer was heard. If this was said of a man whose life was evil, what may we not hope for if we are really humble? — *St Vincent de Paul (1580-1660).*

WHAT, on the other hand, was the lot of the Pharisee? Here was a man praying, fasting and doing many good works, and in spite of all that he was censured by God. Why was this?

Simply because he prided himself on his good works, and took satisfaction out of them as though they were of his own doing.

Here we see a just man lacking humility and declared evil, and a sinner, conscious of his guilt and moved to a real sense of humility, justified because of his lowliness of heart. — *St Vincent de Paul (1580-1660)*.

*   *   *

Our Lord manifests His Truth only to the humble.

CHRIST, the Master of humility, manifests His Truth only to the humble and hides Himself from the proud. — *St Vincent Ferrer (1350-1419)*.

BE careful to give no credit to yourself for anything; if you do, you are stealing from God, to whom alone every good thing is due. — *St Vincent de Paul (1580-1660)*.

A SOUL which exalts itself abases God; but a soul which abases itself exalts God. — *St Augustine (354-430)*.

PRIDE is an illusion, a lie and a theft. And since it is a truth of faith that we are nothing, he who esteems himself and thinks that he is someone is a seducer who deceives himself. — *St John Eudes (1601-80)*.

PRIDE makes us forgetful of our eternal interests. It causes us to neglect totally the care of our soul. — *St John Baptist de la Salle (1651-1719)*.

YOU must ask God to give you power to fight against this sin of pride which is your greatest enemy—the root of all that is evil, and the failure of all that is good. For God resists the proud. — *St Vincent de Paul (1580-1660)*.

★ ★ ★

"Learn of Me," says the Saviour, *"for I am meek and humble of Heart."*

JESUS says *"humble of heart,"* but was He not also humble of mind? Although He was without sin, He humbled Himself like a sinner. He had nothing to be ashamed of. As the good thief put it: *"This Man hath done nothing wrong."*

But we have done everything to be ashamed of. — *St Peter Julian Eymard (1811-68)*.

JESUS invited us to be like Him, humble of heart. But what is humility of the heart?

It consists in receiving humiliations from God with a submissive love, in accepting one's state of life and one's duties whatever they are, and in not being ashamed of one's condition. — *St Peter Julian Eymard (1811-68)*.

WHAT was the life of Christ but a perpetual humiliation? — *St Vincent de Paul (1580-1660)*.

IT was His Will that after His death the Church should give us His image in the crucifix, that He might appear to us in a condition of utmost ignominy. And why? He did it because He knew the worth of humility and the danger of the sin which opposes it. — *St Vincent de Paul (1580-1660)*.

OUR Lord did very few outward things Himself. He willed that His Apostles and Disciples, though they might be poor and ignorant, should be animated by His Spirit, that they might accomplish more than He did. And what was the reason? Clearly that He might set us an example of perfect humility. — *St Vincent de Paul (1580-1660)*.

IF I love Jesus, I ought to resemble Him. If I love Jesus, I ought to love what He loves, what He prefers to all else: humility. — *St Peter Julian Eymard (1811-68)*.

WHAT will be the crown of those who, humble within and humiliated without, have imitated the humility of our Saviour in all its fullness!— *St Bernadette (1844-79)*.

* * *

THERE is something in humility that strangely exalts the heart. — *St Augustine (354-430)*.

To be plunged in humility is to be plunged in God. — *Blessed John Ruysbroeck (1293-1381)*.

IT is by humility that the Lord allows Himself to be conquered, so that He will do all we ask of Him. — *St Teresa of Avila (1515-82)*.

* * *

LET us not deceive ourselves. If we have not got humility, we have nothing. — *St Vincent de Paul (1580-1660)*.

PRAYER

O JESUS! When you were on earth you said: "*Learn of Me, for I am meek and humble of heart, and you shall find rest to your souls*" (*Matt. 11. 29*).

O Almighty King of Heaven! My soul indeed finds rest in seeing Thee condescend to wash the feet of Thy Apostles, "*having taken the form of a slave*" (*Phil. 2. 7*). I recall the words You uttered to teach me the practise of humility: "*I have given you an example, that as I have done to you, so you do also. The servant is not greater than his Lord . . . If you know these things, you shall be blessed if you do them*" (*John 13. 15, 17*).

I understand, dear Lord, these words which come from Thy meek and humble Heart, and I wish to put them into practice with the help of Thy grace.

I desire to humble myself in all sincerity. I implore Thee, dear Jesus, to send me a humiliation whensoever I try to set myself above others.

And yet, dear Lord, you know my weakness. Each morning I resolve to be humble, and in the evening I recognize that I have often been guilty of pride. The sight of these faults tempts me to discouragement. Yet I know that discouragement itself is a form of pride. I wish, therefore, O my God, to build all my trust upon Thee. As Thou canst do all things, deign to implant in my soul this virtue which I desire. And to obtain it from Thy Infinite Mercy, I will often say to Thee: "*Jesus, meek and humble of Heart, make my heart like unto Thine.*" — *St Thérèse of Lisieux (1873-97).*

8

THE CHALLENGE OF CHASTITY

IT is impossible to win the crown without mastering the flesh. — *St Gregory the Great (d. 604).*

★ ★ ★

Christ Himself has elevated this sublime virtue of Chastity to the highest degree. "Blessed are the clean of heart," He says, *"for they shall see God."*

CHASTITY, or cleanness of heart, holds a glorious and distinguished place among the virtues, because she alone enables man to see God; hence Truth Itself said: *"Blessed are the pure in heart, for they shall see God."* — *St Augustine (354-430).*

EVERY virtue in your soul is a precious ornament which makes you dear to God and to man. But holy purity, the queen of virtues, the angelic virtue, is a jewel so precious that those who possess it become like the angels of God in Heaven, even though clothed in mortal flesh. — *St John Bosco (1815-88).*

CHASTITY is the lily among virtues and makes men almost equal to angels. — *St Francis de Sales (1567-1622).*

CHASTITY is the longed for house of Christ and the earthly heaven of the heart. — *St John Climacus (d. 649).*

THE pure soul is a beautiful rose, and the Three Divine Persons descend from Heaven to inhale its fragrance. — *St John Vianney (1786-1859)*.

THOSE whose hearts are pure are the temples of the Holy Spirit. — *St Lucy (d. 304)*.

PURITY means that we put on the likeness of God, as far as is humanly possible. — *St John Climacus (d. 649)*.

PURITY is a supernatural denial of nature, which means that a mortal and corruptible body is rivalling the celestial spirits in a truly marvellous way. — *St John Climacus (d. 649)*.

A PURE soul is like a fine pearl. As long as it is hidden in the shell at the bottom of the sea, no one thinks of admiring it. But if you bring it into the sunshine, this pearl will shine and attract all eyes. Thus, the pure soul which is hidden from the eyes of the world, will one day shine before the angels in the sunshine of eternity. — *St John Vianney (1786-1859)*.

And yet...

How little is purity known in the world. How little we value it. What little care we take to preserve it; what little zeal we have in asking God for it, since we cannot have it of ourselves. — *St John Vianney (1786-1859)*.

THE Holy Ghost tells us that this ugly sin of impurity has covered the whole surface of the earth. — *St John Vianney (1786-1859)*.

O GOD! How many souls does this sin drag down to Hell! — *St John Vianney (1786-1859)*.

LUST served became a custom, and custom not resisted became necessity. — *St Augustine (354-430)*.

THE thought follows the look; delight comes after the thought; and consent after delight. — *St Augustine (354-430)*.

THE thought which is not rejected produces pleasure.
Pleasure leads to consent.
Consent, to action.
Action, to habit.
Habit, to a kind of necessity.
And necessity, to eternal death. — *St Bernard (1090-1153)*.

PLEASURE is momentary, but the punishment due to it is eternal. — *St Gregory Nazianzen (329-90)*.

THOSE who perish, perish by their own negligence. — *St Ambrose (340-97)*.

* * *

Dangers surround us on all sides...

IT is in the theatres that the demon of impurity displays his pomps with greatest advantage. Nothing can be more opposed to the spirit of Christianity, which is a spirit of purity, prayer and penance. — *St John Baptist de la Salle (1651-1719)*.

NOTHING can be more dangerous than evil companions. They communicate the infection of their vices to all who associate with them. — *St John Baptist de la Salle (1651-1719)*.

WHAT could be more out of keeping with our holy religion than impure language? It outrages God. It scandalizes our neighbour. Can a Christian really afford to occupy his mind with such horrible images? A Christian who has been sanctified by contact with the most Adorable Body and Precious Blood of Jesus Christ. — *St John Vianney (1786-1859).*

In a world that is fast losing every moral restraint, the life of a Christian daily becomes more difficult to live. We should take well to heart the warnings and the advice given us by the Saints.

These words will serve as a guide through the moral jungle we are traversing these days.

To abstain from sinful actions is not sufficient for the fulfilment of God's law. The very desire of what is forbidden is evil. — *St John Baptist de la Salle (1651-1719).*

AN evil thought defiles the soul when it is deliberate and is consented to. Our Lord placed evil thoughts at the head of all crimes, because they are their principle and source. — *St John Baptist de la Salle (1651-1719).*

WHEN an evil thought is presented to the mind, we must immediately endeavour to turn our thoughts to God, or to something which is indifferent. But the best rule is, instantly to invoke the names of Jesus and Mary, and to continue to invoke them until the temptation ceases. — *St Alphonsus Liguori (1696-1787).*

IF you wish to prevent all evil thoughts, let your eyes be modestly reserved, and make a league with them never to look upon anything which is not permitted you to desire. — *St Gregory of Nyssa (d. 395).*

GUARD your eyes that they may not look upon anything contrary to purity; your ears, that they may not listen to evil conversation; your mind, by banishing from it all suggestive thoughts; your heart, by stifling impure desires at their very birth. — *St John Baptist de la Salle (1651-1719).*

* * *

HE who has resolved to contend with his flesh and conquer it himself struggles in vain. For unless the Lord destroys the house of the flesh and builds the house of the soul, the man who desires to destroy it has watched and fasted in vain. — *St John Climacus (d. 649).*

CHASTITY is a virtue which we do not have strength to practise unless God gives it to us, and God does not give this strength except to someone who asks for it. But whoever prays for it will certainly obtain it. — *St Alphonsus Liguori (1696-1787).*

TAKE to heart the warning of our Lord: "*But this kind of sin (impurity) is not overcome but by prayer and fasting.*" — *St John Bosco (1815-88).*

ST JAMES tells us that this virtue comes from Heaven and that we shall never have it unless we ask it of God. We should, therefore, frequently ask God to give us purity in our eyes, in our speech, and in all our actions. — *St John Vianney (1786-1859).*

VIGILANCE and prayer are the safeguards of chastity. "*Watch and pray that you enter not into temptation*" (Mark 14. 38).

You should pray often and fervently to be preserved from temptations against purity, and for the grace to overcome them. — *St John Baptist de la Salle (1651-1719)*.

PRAYER is the bulwark of chastity. — *St Gregory the Great (d. 604)*.

As soon as you are tempted to impurity, endeavour to think of the Passion of the Saviour of the world and make the following act: "*My God is nailed to a cross, and shall I consent to these unlawful pleasures?*" — *St Bernard (1090-1153)*.

As soon as lust assails us, let us instantly say: "*Lord, assist me, do not permit me to offend you.*" — *St Jerome (342-420)*.

THE devil, who aims at nothing less than our destruction, never ceases to increase the storm, to overwhelm us by it if he can. — *St Jerome (342-420)*.

WHEN the temptation is violent, it is useful to renew our purpose of never consenting to any sin, saying: "*My God, I wish to die rather than offend Thee. My Jesus, help me; Mary, pray for me.*" — *St Alphonsus Liguori (1696-1787)*.

As water extinguishes fire, so prayer extinguishes the heat of the passions. — *St John Chrysostom (347-407)*.

THE names of Jesus and Mary have special power to banish the temptations of the devil. — *St Alphonsus Liguori (1696-1787)*.

* * *

IF you desire to be chaste, be retired, be modest, be mortified. — *St Leonard of Port Maurice (1676-1751)*.

THE principal safeguard is a prudent reserve, and the not allowing liberties to be taken with you. Purity is a precious jewel, and the owner of a precious stone would never dream of making a display of his riches in the presence of thieves. — *St John Bosco (1815-88)*.

THERE is no remedy so powerful against the heat of concupiscence as the remembrance of our Saviour's Passion. In all my difficulties, I never found anything so efficacious as the wounds of Christ. In them I sleep secure. From them, I derive new life. — *St Augustine (354-430)*.

HE who is chaste in the flesh should not be proud. For he should know that he owes the gift of continence to Another. — *St Clement of Alexandria (d. c. 215)*.

PURITY is the special reward of being humble. — *St John Bosco (1815-88)*.

HUMILITY is the safeguard of chastity. In the matter of purity, there is no greater danger than not fearing danger. When a person puts himself in an occasion, saying, "*I shall not fall*"—it is an almost infallible sign that he will fall, and with great injury to his soul. — *St Philip Neri (1515-95)*.

As a tower defends a camp, so does humility of heart guard the chastity of the body. — *St Anthony of Padua (1195-1231)*.

THROUGHOUT your life, do not trust your body. Place no reliance on it until you stand before the judgment seat of Christ. — *St John Climacus (d. 649)*.

WE can gain nothing from God but by purity, and by holiness. God does great things only by pure souls. He

listens only to the prayers of the innocent or the contrite.
— *St Peter Julian Eymard (1811-68)*.

WHERE Christ is, there modesty is found. — *St Gregory Nazianzen (329-90)*.

IT is he who, after having broken down the ramparts of his passions, ascends with force to the Kingdom of Heaven. — *St Gregory the Great (d. 604)*.

WE must be pure.

I do not speak merely of the purity of the senses. We must observe great purity in our will, in our intentions, in all our actions.

To possess purity of life — in this, all consists. — *St Peter Julian Eymard (1811-68)*.

PRAYER

DEIGN, O Immaculate Virgin, Mother most pure, to accept the loving cry of praise which we send up to thee from the depths of our hearts. Though they can but add little to thy glory, O Queen of Angels, thou dost not despise, in thy love, the praises of the humble and the poor.

Cast down upon us a glance of mercy, O most glorious Queen: graciously receive our petitions. Through thy immaculate purity of body and mind, which rendered thee so pleasing to God, inspire us with a love of innocence and purity.

Teach us to guard carefully the gifts of grace, striving ever after sanctity, so that, being made like unto the image of thy beauty, we may be worthy to become the sharers of thy eternal happiness. Amen. — *St Paschasius (d. 860)*.

9

IN TEMPTATION

THE greatest of all evils is not to be tempted, because there are then grounds for believing that the devil looks upon us as his property. — *St John Vianney (1786-1859)*.

⋆ ⋆ ⋆

Temptations are necessary. Even Christ submitted to them...

IT is necessary that temptations should happen; for who shall be crowned but he that shall lawfully have fought, and how shall a man fight if there be none to attack him? — *St Bernard (1090-1153)*.

HE who with his whole heart draws near unto God must of necessity be proved by temptation and trial. — *St Albert the Great (d. 1280)*.

IF thou art never tempted, thou wilt never be crowned. Is it not, then, better to be tempted and crowned, than, not having been tempted, to be a reprobate? — *St Augustine (354-430)*.

VIRTUE is nothing without the trial of temptation, for there is no conflict without an enemy, no victory without a strife. — *St Leo the Great (d. 461)*.

THE devil only tempts those souls that wish to abandon sin and those that are in a state of grace. The others belong to him: he has no need to tempt them. — *St John Vianney (1786-1859)*.

Those striving for sanctity have to endure greater temptations.

THE tempter, ever on the watch, wages war most violently against those whom he sees most careful to avoid sin. — *St Leo the Great (d. 461)*.

Nevertheless...

THE devil is only permitted to tempt thee as much as is profitable for thy exercise and trial, and in order that thou, who didst not know thyself, mayest find out what thou art. — *St Augustine (354-430)*.

* * *

Well has the life of a Christian been likened to that of a soldier. The spiritual battle to overcome our temptations will go on inexorably till the day we die.

THE spiritual combat in which we kill our passions to put on the new man is the most difficult struggle of all. We must never weary of this combat, but fight the holy fight fervently and perseveringly. — *St Nilus (d. 1004)*.

WE must be much more ardent in bringing the inner man into subjection than in mortifying the body; in breaking the movements of the soul than in breaking bones. It is more difficult to tame the spirit than to lacerate the flesh. — *St Ignatius Loyola (1491-1556)*.

As long as we dwell in the tabernacle of this body and are clothed in this frail flesh, we can moderate our passions, but we cannot cut them off entirely. — *St Jerome (342-420)*.

THE devil flatters that he may deceive us; he charms that he may injure us; he allures that he may slay us. — *St John Climacus (d. 649)*.

BELIEVE me, vices which have been cut down sprout forth anew. When driven away, they return. When extinguished, they are again enkindled. When lulled to sleep, they wake up afresh. — *St Bernard (1090-1153)*.

* * *

The Saints then, were human like ourselves. But they rose manfully to fight their temptations with a determination which we can well make our own.

When thy passions rebel, do thou rebel against them. When they fight, do thou fight them. When they attack thee, do thou attack them. Only beware lest they conquer thee. — *St Augustine (354-430)*.

Go down into the abyss, you evil appetites! I will drown you lest I myself be drowned! — *St Jerome (342-420)*.

As the pilot of a vessel is tried in the storm; as the wrestler is tried in the ring; the soldier in the battle, and the hero in adversity: so is the Christian tried in temptation. — *St Basil (329-79)*.

THE more you are tempted, the more must you persevere in prayer. — *Blessed Angela of Foligno (d. 1309).*

HOWEVER great the temptation, if we knew how to use the weapon of prayer well, we shall come off conquerors at last; for prayer is more powerful than all the devils. — *St Bernard (1090-1183).*

WHEN you are tormented by any passion or evil inclination, if you be so weak as to yield to it, and let it lead you, take it for a certain truth, that it will take deeper root, and wage a more violent war against you. But if you resist it courageous y at first, it will daily diminish. Every day it will have less strength to act upon you, till at length, it will come to have none at all. — *St Dorotheus (d. 362?).*

A MAN who governs his passions is master of the world. We must either command them, or be enslaved by them. It is better to be a hammer than an anvil. — *St Dominic (1170-1221).*

* * *

From their hard won battles against temptation, the Saints, like veteran soldiers, turn to warn us of the dangers and difficulties ahead.

AVOID idleness, loose living companions, immodest talk, and more than all, evil occasions, especially where there is danger of incontinency. — *St Alphonsus Liguori (1696-1787).*

IDLENESS begets a life of discontent. It develops self-love, which is the cause of all our miseries, and renders us unworthy to receive the favours of divine love. — *St Ignatius Loyola (1491-1556).*

A PERSON cannot be too cautious in keeping his eyes from dwelling on dangerous objects. If one does not avoid the voluntary occasions of sin, especially those which have frequently proved fatal to his innocence, it is morally impossible to persevere in the grace of God. *"He that loves the danger shall perish in it" (Ecclus. 3. 27).* — *St Alphonsus Liguori (1696-1787).*

OUR own evil inclinations are far more dangerous than any external enemies. — *St Ambrose (340-97).*

OCCUPY your minds with good thoughts, or the enemy will fill them with bad ones. Unoccupied, they cannot be. — *St Thomas More (1478-1535).*

TAKE heed not to meddle in things which do not concern you, nor even allow them to pass through your mind; for perhaps you will not then be able to fulfil your own task. — *St John of the Cross (1542-91).*

TAKE care not to give way to drunkenness, because this sin so disgraces mankind, that it lowers them beneath the unreasoning animal. — *St Thomas Aquinas (1225-74).*

FAMILIARITY with sinners is, as it were, a hook which draws us to communicate in their vices. Let us avoid evil companions, lest by their company we may be drawn to a communion of vice. — *St Augustine (354-430).*

To know whom to avoid is a great means of saving our souls. — *St Thomas Aquinas (1225-74).*

RUN from places of sin as from the plague. — *St John Climacus (d. 649).*

* * *

DISMISS all anger and look into yourself a little. Remember that he of whom you are speaking is your brother, and, as he is in the way of salvation, God can make him a Saint, in spite of his present weakness. — *St Thomas of Villanova (1488-1555)*.

WHEN you feel the assaults of passion and anger, then is the time to be silent as Jesus was silent in the midst of His ignominies and sufferings. — *St Paul of the Cross (1694-1775)*.

WHEN we have to reply to anyone who has insulted us, we should be careful to do it always with gentleness. A soft answer extinguishes the fire of wrath. — *St Alphonsus Liguori (1696-1787)*.

NOTHING restrains anger, curbs pride, heals the wound of malice, bridles self-indulgence, quenches the passions, checks avarice and puts unclean thoughts to flight, as does the name of Jesus. — *St Bernard (1090-1183)*.

* * *

As long as a single passion reigns in our hearts, though all the others should have been overcome, the soul will never enjoy peace. — *St Joseph Calasanctius (1556-1648)*.

GOD is to be feared in public; to be feared in private. Go in where thou wilt; He sees thee. Light thy lamp; He sees thee. Quench its light; He sees thee. Fear Him who ever beholds thee. If thou wilt sin, seek a place where He cannot see thee, and then do what thou wilt. — *St Augustine (354-430)*.

IT often happens that we pray God to deliver us from some dangerous temptation, and yet God does not hear us but permits the temptation to continue troubling us. In such a case, let us understand that God permits even this for our greater good. When a soul in temptation recommends itself to God, and by His aid resists, O how it then advances in perfection. — *St Alphonsus Liguori (1696-1787).*

This struggle is beautifully illustrated in the following words:

FOR our Lord is there quite close to us, looking on us with kindness, smiling at us and saying: "*So you do love Me!*" — *St John Vianney (1786-1859).*

* * *

We have seen that the most effective counter to temptation is prayer.

To further strengthen our souls, the Saints tell us that the practice of the virtues is essential. Especially the virtue contrary to the vice which assails us.

UNLESS you strive after virtues and practise them, you will never grow to be more than dwarfs. — *St Teresa of Avila (1515-82).*

GRASP with courage every means to advance in virtue and to persevere to the end. — *St Angela Merici (1470-1540).*

BY the perfect exercise of only one virtue, a person may attain to the height of all the rest. — *St Gregory Nazianzen (329-90).*

WHOEVER practises one virtue perfectly must possess every other virtue.

We should choose a virtue now for special devotion. — *St Bridget of Kildare (450-525)*.

IF it were given a man to see virtue's reward in the next world, he would occupy his intellect, memory and will in nothing but good works, careless of danger or fatigue. — *St Catherine of Genoa (1447-1510)*.

* * *

We are further advised to have frequent recourse to spiritual reading. The graces granted us through the reading of the Scriptures and pious books buttress our souls against temptations.

WHY do you not use the time when you have nothing to do for reading or for prayer? Why do you not go and visit Christ our Lord and speak with Him and listen to Him? For when we pray we speak with God, and when we read, we listen to God. — *St Ambrose (340-97)*.

THERE is no doubt that through the reading of the Sacred Scriptures the soul is set aflame in God and becomes purified from all vices. — *St Jerome (342-420)*.

YOU will not see anyone who is really striving after his advancement who is not given to spiritual reading. And as to him who neglects it, the fact will soon be observed in his progress. — *St Athanasius (297-373)*.

LET sacred reading be the life of the soul. — *St Ambrose (340-97)*.

* * *

Finally, we should never cease to pray for the necessary grace which will enable us to triumph over every difficulty.

LET us ask for Divine grace. He who asks for anything else asks for nothing; not because all things are nothing, but because, in comparison of such a thing, all else that can be desired is nothing at all. — *St Augustine (354-430)*.

WHO is so strong as never to be overcome by temptation, except he who has the grace of the Lord for his helper? — *St Augustine (354-430)*.

IT is impossible for a soul to cross the dreadful ocean of sins, and to keep God's commandments and be saved, unless it is aided by the Spirit of Jesus Christ and borne along in the vessel of Divine grace. — *St Macarius (314-35)*.

GRACE prevents the wicked, that he may become just. It follows the just, that he may not become wicked. — *St Fulgentius (468-533)*.

GRACE will not act without us, in order that we may will to do right. But when we will, it works along with us. Grace prevents him who is not willing, that he may will. It accompanies him who wills, lest he will in vain. — *St Augustine (354-430)*.

GRACE can do nothing without the will and the will can do nothing without grace. — *St John Chrysostom (347-407)*.

GOD inspires us with the beginning of a holy will, and with power and opportunity; and what we have begun well He assists us to accomplish. — *St Prosper of Aquitane (d. 465)*.

IF we have obtained the grace of God, none shall prevail against us, but we shall be stronger than all who oppose us. — *St John Chrysostom (347-407)*.

PRAYER

O SACRED Heart of Jesus! I fly to Thee, I unite myself with Thee, I enclose myself to Thee!

Receive this, my call for help, O my Saviour, as a sign of my horror of all within me contrary to Thy Holy Love. Let me rather die a thousand times than consent!

Be Thou my Strength, O God: defend me, protect me. I am thine, and desire forever to be Thine! Amen. — *St Margaret Mary Alacoque (1647-90)*.

IO

CONTRITION

It is human to fall, but angelic to rise again. — *St Mary Euphrasia Pelletier (1796-1868).*

* * *

Is sin unavoidable?

No one really wants to sin against God, even though we do all sin without being forced to do so. — *St John Climacus (d. 649).*

Let it be assured that to do no wrong is really superhuman, and belongs to God alone. — *St Gregory Nazianzen (329-90).*

To sin is human, but to persist in sin is devilish. — *St Catherine of Siena (1347-80).*

Even so...

Can any sin be called light, since every sin involves some contempt of God? — *St Eucherius (d. 743).*

Every sin is a debt which we contract towards Almighty God, and His justice demands payment down to the very last farthing. — *St Augustine (354-430).*

The body dies when the soul departs; but the soul dies when God departs. — *St Augustine (354-430).*

Is there not an infinite opposition between God and sin?
— *St Pius X (1835-1914)*.

* * *

To sin, as St Catherine of Siena has observed, is human.
But we should repent of it at once and resolve to amend.

WHEN you commit any sin, repent of it at once and resolve to amend. If it is a grievous sin, confess it as soon
as possible. — *St Alphonsus Liguori (1696-1787)*.

HE who falls into sin, however light it may be, ought to
rise immediately, have recourse to God, beg pardon of
Him, and ask grace never to commit it again. —
St Aloysius Gonzaga (1568-91).

Do not imitate those who deceive themselves by saying:
"I will sin and then go to confession." How do you know
that you will have time to make your confession? Is it
not madness to wound oneself, in the hope that a doctor
will be found who will heal the wound? — *St John
Bosco (1815-88)*.

SHOULD we fall into sin, let us at once humble ourselves
sorrowfully in His presence, and then, with an act of
unbounded confidence, let us throw ourselves into the
ocean of His goodness, where every failing will be can-
celled and anxiety will be turned into love. — *St Paul
of the Cross (1694-1775)*.

IF my conscience were burdened with all the sins it is
possible to commit, I would still go and throw myself
into our Lord's arms, my heart all broken up with contrition. I know what tenderness He has for any prodigal
child of His that comes back to Him.— *St Thérèse of
Lisieux (1873-97)*.

EVEN though I had committed but one little sin, I should have ample reason to repent of it all my life. — *St Francis of Assisi (1181-1226)*.

* * *

The Sacrament of Penance heals, justifies and grants pardon of sin.
All our hope consists in this.

CONFESSION heals, confession justifies, confession grants pardon of sin. All hope consists in confession. In confession there is a chance for mercy. Believe it firmly. Do not doubt, do not hesitate, never despair of the mercy of God. Hope and have confidence in confession. — *St Isidore of Seville (d. 636)*.

THE confessor is the doctor of the soul. — *St Dominic Savio (1842-57)*.

* * *

We should contemplate in spirit the dying Saviour on the Cross, His arms outspread as if to embrace the penitent.
The following words were uttered by a Saint holding up a crucifix to the multitude and exorting them to cast all their hope in God's mercy.

THIS is a Friend who will not terrify you, who will not abandon you. Hope in Him, and Heaven is yours! — *St Joseph Cafasso (1811-60)*.

TAKE the holy crucifix in your hands, kiss its wounds with great love, and ask Him to preach you a sermon.
Listen to what the thorns, the nails, and that Divine Blood say to you. Oh! What a sermon. — *St Paul of the Cross (1694-1775)*.

THE crucifix is the book of books, the first book. Before the crucifix we feel true sorrow for sin and fixing our gaze on it we also feel the greatest comfort. — *St Mary Joseph Rossello (1811-80)*.

WHO will dare to measure, by the greatness of his sins, the immensity of that infinite mercy which casts them all into the depths of the sea of oblivion, when we repent of them with love? — *St Francis de Sales (1567-1622)*.

GOD's mercy is like an unleashed torrent; it bears away all hearts in its flood? — *St John Vianney (1786-1859)*.

AFTER confession, thank Almighty God for the pardon which you hope to have received, and renew your good resolution never more to offend Him, and to avoid all occasions of sin; and pray to Jesus and Mary for perseverance. — *St Alphonsus Liguori (1696-1787)*.

REPENTANCE is the renewal of Baptism and a contract with God for a second life. — *St John Climacus (d. 649)*.

* * *

We must remember to make the necessary satisfaction for past sins and firmly resolve to avoid in future the dangerous occasions of sin which have been the cause of our fall.

SATISFACTION consists in the cutting off of the causes of the sin. Thus, fasting is the proper antidote to lust; prayer to pride, to envy, anger and sloth; alms to covetousness. — *St Richard of Chichester (d. 1253)*.

IT is necessary, too, that we shun the occasions which have been the cause of our sin. We must have recourse to fervent prayer, receive frequently and worthily the sacraments. He who does this will be sure to persevere. — *St John Vianney (1786-1859)*.

OF all the counsels of Christ, one of the greatest, and so to say, the foundation of religion, is to fly the occasions of sin. — *St Bernardine of Siena (1380-1444)*.

HE who walks along a precipice, although he may not fall over, yet he trembles and often falls through that very fear. Even so, he who flies not far from sin, but keeps near to it, lives in continual fear, and often falls. — *St John Chrysostom (347-407)*.

THAT hope is deceitful which hopes to be saved amidst the occasions of sin. — *St Augustine (354-430)*.

YOU ought to make every effort to free yourselves even from venial sin, and to do what is most perfect. — *St Teresa of Avila (1515-82)*.

BE assured that he who shall always walk faithfully in God's presence, always ready to give Him an account of all his actions, shall never be separated from Him by consenting to sin. — *St Thomas Aquinas (1225-74)*.

* * *

We must do violence to ourselves...

IF we wish to save our souls, we must resolve to do violence to ourselves. *"The Kingdom of Heaven suffereth violence, and the violent bear it away"* (Matt. 11. 12). He who does not do violence to himself will not be saved. — *St Alphonsus Liguori (1696-1787)*.

HE will be a Saint if he be truly mortified. — *St Francis Borgia (1510-72)*.

THE perfection of a Christian consists in mortifying himself for the love of Christ. To mortify one's passions, however small, is a greater help in the spiritual life than many abstinences and fasts. — *St Philip Neri (1515-95)*.

WE should perform our penance overwhelmed with joy at being able to satisfy God, whom we have offended, and at finding such an easy means of effacing our sins which should have earned eternal sufferings for us. — *St John Vianney (1786-1859)*.

* * *

The Saints have given us a very detailed explanation of practical mortification and penance. We would be wrong, as the following counsels clearly reveal, to picture the Saints as a group of individuals wholly given up to heroic and unheard of sacrifices. They generally lived on a level with ourselves, and we can easily tread the path they have paved for us below.

HE renounces himself, and takes up his cross, who, from having been unchaste becomes chaste; from having been immoderate becomes temperate; from having been weak and timid becomes strong and courageous. — *St Jerome (342-420)*.

IN the first place, the eyes must be mortified. We must abstain from looking at any object that may give occasion to temptation. — *St Alphonsus Liguori (1696-1787)*.

WE must also mortify our tongue, by abstaining from words of detraction, abuse, and obscenity. An impure word spoken in jest may prove a scandal to others, and sometimes a word of double meaning, said in a witty way, does more harm than a word openly impure. — *St Alphonsus Liguori (1696-1787)*.

THE taste must also be mortified. Intemperance in eating and drinking is often the cause of incontinency. — *St Alphonsus Liguori (1696-1787).*

FINALLY, we must mortify our hearing and our touch: the hearing by avoiding listening to scandalous conversations: the touch, by using all possible caution towards others as also with ourselves. — *St Alphonsus Liguori (1696-1787).*

YOU should bear patiently the bad temper of other people, the slights, the rudeness that may be offered you. Endure without complaining, the heat, the cold, the wind, the rain. When you are weary, don't give way to bad temper yourself. Bear any illness with resignation, even thanksgiving to God in your heart. — *St John Bosco (1815-88).*

SUFFER and offer up those trifling injuries, those petty inconveniences, that daily befall you. This toothache, this headache, this cold, this contempt or that scorn.

All these small sacrifices, being accepted and embraced with love, are highly pleasing to the Divine goodness, who for a single cup of cold water has promised a sea of perfect bliss for His faithful. — *St Francis de Sales (1567-1622).*

MISS no single opportunity of making some small sacrifice, here by a smiling look, there by a kindly word; always doing the smallest things right, and doing it all for love. — *St Thérèse of Lisieux (1873-97).*

BE assured that mortification of the senses is far more profitable than wearing even sharp chains or hair shirts. — *St Francis de Sales (1567-1622).*

BELIEVE me, the writing of pious books, the composing of the sublimest poetry; all that does not equal the smallest act of self-denial. — *St Thérèse of Lisieux (1873-97).*

The Saints caution us that failure to practise some degree of self-restraint in life may well lead to disastrous consequences.

HE who knows not how to command his desires, finds himself hurried away with them. — *St Ambrose (340-97).*

THE more we indulge ourselves in soft living and pamper our bodies, the more rebellious they will become against the spirit. — *St Rita of Cascia (1381-1457).*

We are again reminded that extremes of penance as practised by the ascetics and desert hermits are certainly not intended for modern sanctity.

IF you wish to go to extremes, let it be in sweetness, patience, humility and charity. — *St Philip Neri (1515-95).*

ONE should never deny the body what is due to it, that the body itself may not hinder what is due to the soul. — *St Peter of Alcantara (1499-1562).*

REMEMBER that sacrifice exists in the will; and although force of habit may dull the sting of sacrifice, the merit lasts and increases with the repetition of the sacrifice. — *St Peter Julian Eymard (1811-68).*

LAMENT and consider that day lost in which you have not in some way mortified yourself for the love of God. — *St Mary Magdalen of Pazzi (1566-1607).*

THE more we have denied ourselves during the day, the nearer are we each evening to the Heart of our Lord. — *St Madeleine Sophie Barat (1779-1865).*

* * *

Besides making satisfaction for our own sins, we should also be mindful of making atonement for the sins of the whole world.

No sacrifice is more acceptable to God than zeal for souls. — *St Gregory the Great (d. 604).*

IT is only by sacrifice and suffering, offered as penance, that you will be able, by the grace of God, to convert sinners. — *St John Vianney (1786-1859).*

ONE just soul can obtain pardon for a thousand sinners. — *St Margaret Mary Alacoque (1647-90).*

ONE soul saved is worth more than our lives. — *St Madeleine Sophie Barat (1779-1865).*

IF I succeed in saving only a single soul, I can be sure that my own will be saved. — *St Dominic Savio (1842-57).*

THE world is so wicked that there is almost greater need of reparation than of thanksgiving. — *St Peter Julian Eymard (1811-68).*

I WOULD give.my life a thousand times that God might not be offended. — *St Gerard Majella (1726-55).*

I SHOULD willingly give every drop of my blood to please Him and to prevent sinners offending Him. I shall be satisfied only when I am a victim, to make reparation for my innumerable sins and for the sins of all the world. — *St Gemma Galgani (1878-1903)*.

O MY God! Would I might prevent all from offending Thee! Rather, would I could make Thee known, loved and served by all Thy creatures! This is the sole object of my desire, for all things else are unworthy of attention. — *St Anthony Mary Claret (1807-70)*.

OF all divine things, the most godlike is to co-operate with God in the conversion of sinners. —*St Denis the Areopagite (1st Century)*.

BUT since all your satisfactions and penances are too small and deficient to atone for so many sins, unite them to those of your Saviour Jesus lifted up upon the Cross. Receive His Divine Blood as it flows from His wounds, and offer It up to appease Divine justice. Unite your reparation to that of the most Blessed Virgin at the foot of the Cross and from the love of Jesus for His Mother, you will obtain everything. — *St Peter Julian Eymard (1811-68)*.

PRAYER

PARDON me, O perfections of my God, for having preferred imperfect and evil inclinations to Thee!

Pardon me, O justice of my God, for having outraged Thee by my sins!

Pardon me, O holiness of my God, for having so long stained Thy sight's purity by my sins!

Pardon me, O mercy of my God, for having despised so long Thy mercy's voice!

In deep sorrow and contrition, I cast myself at Thy feet: Have mercy on me. Amen. — *St Ignatius Loyola (1491-1556)*.

II

THE BREAD OF LIFE

HOLY Communion is the shortest and the safest way to Heaven. — *St Pius X (1835-1914)*.

★ ★ ★

The Holy Eucharist is the supreme proof of God's love for man.

SINCE Christ Himself has said: "*This is My Body*"— who shall dare to doubt that It is His Body? — *St Cyril of Jerusalem (315-86)*.

As by the Word of God, Jesus our Saviour was made Flesh and had both Flesh and Blood for our salvation, so also the food which has been blessed by the word of prayer instituted by Him is both the Flesh and Blood of Jesus Incarnate. — *St Justin, Martyr (d. 165)*.

THIS is the Bread of everlasting life which supports the substance of our soul. — *St Ambrose (340-97)*.

THE Holy Eucharist is the perfect expression of the love of Jesus Christ for man, since It is the quintessence of all the mysteries of His Life. — *St Peter Julian Eymard (1811-68)*.

THE Blessed Eucharist is the perfect Sacrament of the Lord's Passion, since It contains Christ Himself and His Passion. — *St Thomas Aquinas (1225-74)*.

★ ★ ★

83

IN all He did from the Incarnation to the Cross, the end Jesus Christ had in mind was the gift of the Eucharist, His personal and corporal union with each Christian, through Communion.

He saw in It the means of communicating to us all the treasures of His Passion, all the virtues of His Sacred Humanity, and all the merits of His Life. — *St Peter Julian Eymard (1811-68)*.

The Eucharist was instituted for us, to satisfy the great love which Christ bore for us in His Sacred Heart.

THE Eucharist is in excess of what was required for the work of Redemption. It was not demanded of Jesus Christ by His Father's Justice. Why then did our Lord institute the Eucharist?

He instituted It for Himself, to satisfy Himself, to content His Heart.

Understood in this light, the Eucharist is a most divine, tender and loving thing: goodness and overflowing tenderness are Its character and nature. — *St Peter Julian Eymard (1811-68)*.

*   *   *

Holy Communion is the short-cut to Heaven.

HOLY Communion is the shortest and the safest way to Heaven.

There are others:

Innocence, for instance, but that is for little children.

Penance, but we are afraid of it.

Generous endurance of the trials of life, but when they come we weep and ask to be spared.

The surest, easiest, shortest way is by the Eucharist. — *St Pius X (1835-1914)*.

THE Flesh of Jesus is the Flesh of Mary, and the Saviour gives us this Flesh of Mary as the nourishment of our salvation. — *St Augustine (354-430)*.

OUR Lord does not come down from Heaven every day to lie in a golden ciborium. He comes to find another heaven which is infinitely dearer to Him—the heaven of our souls, created in His Image, the living temples of the Adorable Trinity. — *St Thérèse of Lisieux (1873-97)*.

Do you realize that Jesus is there in the tabernacle expressly for you, for *you* alone?

He burns with the desire to come into your heart.— *St Thérèse of Lisieux (1873-97)*.

HUMILITY was extolled by Christ; and surely in this Sacrament He preaches an unrivalled humility, which disdains no dwelling, but consents to come like a guest to any heart, even one that is defiled. — *St Thomas Aquinas (1225-74)*.

IN this dark vale of tears, I wish solely to feed upon this secret manna, this delicious substance. — *St Cajetan (1480-1547)*.

*   *   *

A SOUL can do nothing that is more pleasing to God than to communicate in a state of grace. — *St Alphonsus Liguori (1696-1787)*.

THE Last Supper lasted about three hours. It was the passion of His Love.

That Bread was so expensive!

People say, "Bread is dear", but what is that in comparison with the price of heavenly Bread, the Bread of Life?

Let us therefore eat this Bread; It is ours, our Lord bought It for us and paid for It Himself. He gives It to us; we have but to take It. What an honour! What love! — *St Peter Julian Eymard (1811-68)*.

LOVE tends to union with the object loved. Now Jesus Christ loves a soul that is in a state of grace with an immense love; He ardently desires to unite Himself with it. This is what Holy Communion does. — *St Alphonsus Liguori (1696-1787)*.

THE heart preparing for Communion should be as a crystal vial filled with clear water in which the least mote of uncleanness will be seen. — *Blessed Elizabeth Seton (1774-1821)*.

LET no one approach this holy Table without reverent devotion and fervent love, without true penitence, or without recalling the mystery of his redemption. — *St Thomas Aquinas (1225-74)*.

BEFORE you receive Jesus Christ, you should remove from your heart all worldly attachments which you know to be displeasing to Him. He who wishes to communicate often must empty his heart of the things of earth. — *St Augustine (354-430)*.

THE soul about to receive Holy Communion should be pure, that it may be purified; alive, that it may be quickened; just, that it may be justified; ready, that it may be incorporated with God uncreate who was made Man, and that it may be one with Him unto all eternity. — *Blessed Angela of Foligno (d. 1309)*.

We should pray fervently for the grace to receive the Sacrament worthily. Then we may approach the altar with confidence born of the words of Christ: "Take and eat, this is My Body."

BEG Him, supplicate Him, that He will permit you to receive with true faith. O heavenly bliss! Delight past all expression! How consoling, how sweet, the presence of Jesus to the longing, harassed soul! It is instant peace, and balm to every wound. — *Blessed Elizabeth Seton (1774-1821).*

YOU must also implore our Blessed Lady to lend you her heart, that you may receive her Son there with the same dispositions as her own. If she will come and dwell with you, in order to receive her Son, she can do so by the dominion which she has over all hearts. — *St Louis de Montfort (1673-1716).*

ALTHOUGH you feel tepid, approach with confidence; for the greater your infirmity, the more you stand in need of a physician. — *St Bonaventure (1221-74).*

OF course you are unworthy. But when do you hope to be worthy? You will be no more worthy at the end than at the beginning. All the good works that we could ever do would never make us worthy, in this sense, of Holy Communion. God alone is worthy of Himself, He alone can make us worthy of Him, and He alone can make us worthy with His own worthiness. — *St Catherine of Siena (1347-80).*

WHEN we approach the altar we must, with God's help, prepare ourselves with all our power, and search into every corner of our souls, lest any sin be hidden therein. For, if Christ sees us clothed with the light of charity, He will give us of His Flesh and Blood, not to our condemnation, but to our salvation. — *St Augustine (354-430)*.

WHEREFORE with full assurance let us partake of the Body and Blood of Christ, that thou be made of the same body and blood with Him. For thus we come to bear Christ in us. According to Peter: "*We become partakers of the Divine Nature*" *(2 Peter 1. 4)*. — *St Cyril of Jerusalem (315-86)*.

RECEIVE Him, in whom, by whom, for whom, you believe, hope and love. — *St Francis de Sales (1567-1622)*.

* * *

How does He unite Himself to us in the Eucharist? By the nearest and most intimate union. Our Lord compares it to that which exists between His Father and Himself. "*As the living Father hath sent Me, and I live by the Father: so he that eateth Me, the same also shall live by Me*" *(John 6. 58)*. — *St Ignatius Loyola (1491-1556)*.

JESUS Christ gives Himself entirely to us; He unites His Sacred Body with ours; and, by this union, we become one and the same spirit with Him. As the food which we take nourishes our body, so the Holy Eucharist is the nourishment of our soul. For even as our bodily food is changed into our substance, so the Holy Eucharist transforms us into Jesus Christ. — *St John Baptist de la Salle (1651-1719)*.

IN a union that is true and real, we are transformed into Him. Drinking of the Divine Essence in that sea, one takes into oneself all that one is ever able to receive, for in God all things are found. — *St Charles of Sezze (1613-70)*.

As two pieces of wax fused together make one, so he who receives Holy Communion is so united with Christ that Christ is in him and he is in Christ. — *St Cyril of Alexandria (376-444)*.

UPON receiving Holy Communion, the Adorable Blood of Jesus Christ really flows in our veins and His Flesh is really blended with ours. — *St John Vianney (1786-1859)*.

BY Holy Communion, we are changed into the flesh of Him who became our flesh. — *St Leo the Great (d. 461)*.

WE feed on Thee, Lord, and we drink Thee, not to consume Thee, but to live by Thee. — *St Ephraem (306-73)*.

LET us adore His power, exhausting itself in this act of love. — *St Peter Julian Eymard (1811-68)*.

* * *

DOES He not give Himself whole and entire to each one? And if a greater number come to receive Him, does He divide Himself up? Does He give less to each one? If the church is full of adorers, can they not all pray to Jesus and converse with Him? Is not each one listened to and his prayer granted as if he were the only one in church?

Such is the personal love of Jesus for us. — *St Peter Julian Eymard (1811-68)*.

HE is generous even to exhaustion; and what is most wonderful is, that He gives Himself thus entirely, not once only, but every day, if we wish it. Every fresh

Communion is a new gift which Jesus Christ makes of Himself. — *St Ignatius Loyola (1491-1556)*.

* * *

AFTER Communion, let us not lose so good an opportunity of negotiation. God does not repay with ingratitude the abode in which He is well received. — *St Teresa of Avila (1551-82)*.

THIS Sacrament infuses into the soul great interior peace, a strong inclination to virtue, and great willingness to practise it, thus rendering it easy to walk in the path of perfection. —*St Alphonsus Liguori (1696-1787)*.

JUST as in this world love lives on happiness and desires, so the soul, through the Eucharist, both enjoys and desires at the same time; she eats, and is still hungry. — *St Peter Julian Eymard (1811-68)*.

ONE of the most admirable effects of Holy Communion is to preserve souls from falling, and to help those who fall from weakness to rise again. Therefore, it is much more profitable to approach the divine Sacrament frequently, with love, respect, and confidence, than to keep back from an excess of fear. — *St Ignatius Loyola (1491-1556)*.

The Saints urge us to receive Communion frequently...

IF, whenever Christ's Blood is shed, It is shed for the forgiveness of sins, I, who sin often, should receive It often. I need a frequent remedy. — *St Ambrose (340-97)*.

I MAY say with assurance that the greatest distance the times of communicating, for such as desire to serve God devoutly, should not exceed a month. — *St Francis de Sales (1567-1622)*.

IF we profit by the grace of frequent Communion, we shall be other Christs. At least, we shall be able to say with St Paul: "*I live, no, not I, but Christ liveth in me.*" — *St Madeleine Sophie Barat (1779-1865)*.

HE who communicates most frequently will be freest from sin, and will make farthest progress in Divine Love. — *St Alphonsus Liguori (1696-1787)*.

WHEREAS in the Lord's Prayer, we are bidden to ask for 'our daily bread', the Holy Fathers of the Church all but unanimously teach that by these words must be understood, not so much that material bread which is the support of the body, as the Eucharistic bread, which ought to be our daily food. — *St Pius X (1835-1914)*.

THIS is our daily Bread; take It daily, that It may profit thee daily. Live, as to deserve to receive It daily. — *St Augustine (354-430)*.

FREQUENT and daily Communion is greatly desired by our Lord and the Church. — *St Pius X (1835-1914)*.

IT is impossible that if one communicates daily, one should not gradually be delivered even from venial sins and from all attachment to them. — *St Pius X (1835-1914)*.

THE Eucharist is necessary to preserve the soul in the spiritual life of grace; for the soul, like the body, becomes gradually exhausted, if care is not taken to repair its strength. — *St John Baptist de la Salle (1651-1719)*.

WHEN the body is deprived of food it languishes and dies; and it is the same with the soul, without the Bread which sustains life. — *Blessed Théophane Vénard (1829-61)*.

THE longer you stay away from Communion, the more your soul will become weak, and in the end you will become dangerously indifferent. — *St John Bosco (1815-88)*.

*   *   *

WITHOUT the Eucharist, Christ's love would be nothing more for us than a lifeless love, a love of the past, which we would quickly forget, and which it would be almost excusable for us to forget.

Love has its laws, its requirements, which the Eucharist alone fully satisfies. — *St Peter Julian Eymard (1811-68)*.

ON account of the Eucharist, Jesus has every right to be loved because in It He gives us a proof of infinite Love. — *St Peter Julian Eymard (1811-68)*.

PRAYER

ANIMA CHRISTI

SOUL of Christ, make me holy.
Body of Christ, save me.
Blood of Christ, possess me completely.
Water from the side of Christ, wash me.
Passion of Christ, strengthen me.
O good Jesus, hear me.
Within Your wounds, hide me.
Suffer me not to be separated from You.
From the wicked enemy defend me.
At the hour of death call me
and bid me come unto You,
that with Your Saints
I may praise You
for ever and ever.
Amen. — *St Ignatius Loyola (1491-1556)*.

12

HEAVEN IN OUR MIDST

GOD in His omnipotence could not give more, in His wisdom He knew not how to give more, in His riches He had not more to give, than the Eucharist. — *St Augustine (354-430).*

* * *

The supreme object of our worship of God is the adoration of His Body, Blood, Soul and Divinity in the Most Holy Eucharist.

THE Blessed Sacrament is the first and supreme object of our worship. We must preserve in the depths of our hearts a constant and uninterrupted, profound adoration of this precious pledge of Divine Love. — *St Mary Euphrasia Pelletier (1796-1868).*

O SACRAMENT of Love! O sign of Unity! O bond of Charity! He who would have Life finds here indeed a Life to live *in* and a Life to live *by*. — *St Augustine (354-430).*

* * *

WHAT induced Jesus Christ to condescend to be present in our churches by day and night?

It was that we might be able to come to Him whenever we wanted to.

What an immense privilege we Christians enjoy. — *St John Vianney (1786-1859)*.

THE churches are always open: all can go to converse with Jesus whenever they wish. He desires that we speak to Him with unbounded confidence. It is for this purpose that He remains under the species of bread. — *St Alphonsus Liguori (1696-1787)*.

How kind is our Sacramental Jesus! He welcomes you at any hour of the day or night. His Love never knows rest. He is always most gentle towards you. When you visit Him, He forgets your sins and speaks only of His joy, His tenderness, and His Love. By the reception He gives to you, one would think He has need of you to make Him happy. — *St Peter Julian Eymard (1811-68)*.

HE loves, He hopes, He waits. If He came down on our altars on certain days only, some sinner, on being moved to repentance, might have to look for Him, and not finding Him, have to wait. Our Lord prefers to wait Himself for the sinner for years rather than keep him waiting one instant.

How few reflect that Jesus loves them that much in the Most Blessed Sacrament. — *St Peter Julian Eymard (1811-68)*.

* * *

GO to Jesus. He loves you and is waiting for you to give you many graces. He is on the altar surrounded by angels adoring and praying. Let them make some room for you and join them in doing what they do. — *St Mary Joseph Rossello (1811-80)*.

DRAW near to our Lord, thoroughly aware of your own nothingness; and you may hope all things from His Goodness and Mercy. Never forget that Jesus Christ is no less powerful, no less generous in the Blessed Sacrament than He was during His mortal life on earth. — *St Mary Euphrasia Pelletier (1796-1868).*

Go to your adoration as one would go to Heaven, to the divine banquet. Tell yourself, "In four hours, in two hours, in one hour, our Lord will give me an audience of grace and love. He has invited me; He is waiting for me; He is longing for me." — *St Peter Julian Eymard (1811-68).*

BE natural in your meditation. Use up your own stock of piety and love before resorting to books. Remember that our good Master prefers the poverty of our heart to the most sublime thoughts borrowed from others. You can be sure our Lord wants *our* heart and not that of someone else. — *St Peter Julian Eymard (1811-68).*

WHEN you are before the altar where Christ reposes, you ought no longer to think that you are amongst men; but believe that there are troops of angels and archangels standing by you, and trembling with respect before the sovereign Master of Heaven and earth. Therefore, when you are in church, be there in silence, fear, and veneration. — *St John Chrysostom (347-407).*

WE can actually come and adore Him like the shepherds; we can prostrate ourselves before Him like the Magi; we need no longer regret our not having been present at Bethlehem or on Calvary. — *St Peter Julian Eymard (1811-68).*

KNEELING before the tabernacle, I can think of only one thing to say to our Lord: "*My God, you know that I love you.*" And I feel that my prayer does not weary Jesus; knowing my weakness, He is satisfied with my good will. — *St Thérèse of Lisieux (1873-97).*

IN order to adore well we must keep in mind that the Holy Eucharist is Jesus Christ past, present and future; that the Eucharist is the last development of the Incarnation and mortal life of our Saviour; that in the Eucharist, Jesus Christ gives us every grace; that all truths tend to and end in the Eucharist, and that there is nothing more to be added when we have said: *"The Eucharist"*, since It is Jesus Christ. — *St Peter Julian Eymard (1811-68).*

WE should consider those moments spent before the Blessed Sacrament as the happiest of our lives. — *St John Vianney (1786-1859).*

* * *

And yet, in spite of this excess of Love, how little is Jesus loved in the Blessed Sacrament! We are told that if our hearts remain insensible to His Presence on the altar, He, the God of Love, is vanquished.

IF the love of Jesus in the Most Blessed Sacrament does not win our hearts, Jesus is vanquished! Our ingratitude is greater than His Goodness; our malice is more powerful than His Charity! — *St Peter Julian Eymard (1811-68).*

ADORE and visit Jesus abandoned and forsaken by men in His Sacrament of love. Man has time for everything except for visits to his Lord and God, who is waiting and longing for him in His tabernacle. The streets and houses of amusement are filled with people. The house of God is deserted. — *St Peter Julian Eymard (1811-68).*

How many insults must Jesus Christ have suffered in this Sacrament, in order to remain with us. Some have trampled on the Sacred Host, and others have thrown It into the mire. He foresaw all these injuries; but still He resolved to remain with us on the altar, that we might not be deprived of His amiable presence. — *St Peter Julian Eymard (1811-68)*.

No tongue can express the greatness of the love which Jesus Christ bears to our souls. He did not wish that between Him and His servants there should be any other pledge than Himself, to keep alive the remembrance of Him. — *St Peter of Alcantara (1499-1562)*.

* * *

Do you want our Lord to give you many graces? Visit Him often. Do you want Him to give you few graces? Visit Him seldom.

Visits to the Blessed Sacrament are powerful and indispensable means of overcoming the attacks of the devil. Make frequent visits to Jesus in the Blessed Sacrament and the devil will be powerless against you. — *St John Bosco (1815-88)*.

EVERY time we come into the presence of the Eucharist we may say: This precious Testament cost Jesus Christ His life. For the Eucharist is a testament, a legacy which becomes valid only at the death of the testator. Our Lord thereby shows us His boundless love, for He Himself said there is no greater proof of love than to lay down one's life for one's friends. — *St Peter Julian Eymard (1811-68)*.

OUR love for the Blessed Sacrament should be carried to the highest degree; the highest degree of love and adoration is the silence which prays and pours itself out in adoration before the grandeur of a hidden God. — *St Mary Euphrasia Pelletier (1796-1868)*.

WE believe in the love of God for us. To believe in love is everything. It is not enough to believe in the Truth. We must believe in Love and Love is our Lord in the Blessed Sacrament.

That is the faith that makes our Lord loved. Ask for this pure and simple faith in the Eucharist. Men will teach you; but only Jesus will give you the grace to believe in Him.

You have the Eucharist. What more do you want?
— *St Peter Julian Eymard (1811-68).*

PRAYER

O GODHEAD hid, devoutly I adore Thee,
Who truly art within the forms before me;
To Thee my heart I bow with bended knee,
As failing quite in contemplating Thee.

Sight, touch and taste in Thee are each deceived;
The ear alone most safely is believed:
I believe all the Son of God has spoken,
Than truth's own word there is no truer token.

God only on the cross lay hid from view;
But here lies hid at once the manhood too:
And I, in both professing my belief,
Make the same prayer as the repentant thief.

Thy wounds, as Thomas saw, I do not see;
Yet Thee confess my Lord and God to be;
Make me believe Thee ever more and more;
In Thee my hope, in Thee my love to store.

Jesus! Whom for the present veil'd I see,
What I so thirst for, O vouchsafe to me:
That I may see Thy countenance unfolding,
And may be blest Thy glory in beholding.
— *St Thomas Aquinas (1225-74).*

13

KEEPING CHRIST IN THE FAMILY

I TURN to you, dear parents, and implore you to imitate the Holy Family of Nazareth. — *St John Vianney (1786-1859).*

★ ★ ★

In these difficult days, the state of marriage requires more constancy than ever before.
There is a crying need for a renewal of the Christian spirit in family life.

THE state of marriage is one that requires more virtue and constancy than any other: it is a perpetual exercise of mortification. — *St Francis de Sales (1567-1622).*

MATRIMONY is a great Sacrament, as St Paul says, but only in Christ and His Holy Church. Husbands, love your wives, as Christ loves His Church: wives, be subject to your husbands, in love and obedience, and care for one another. Bear with your imperfections. — *St John Vianney (1786-1859).*

THE man who wishes to have a happy married life ought to consider the sanctity and dignity of the Sacrament of Matrimony. — *St Francis de Sales (1567-1622).*

ALL the wealth in the world cannot be compared with the happiness of living together happily united. — *Blessed Margaret d'Youville (1701-71).*

IT is a great honour to you who are married that God, in His design to multiply souls who may bless and praise Him for all eternity, causes you to co-operate with Him in so noble a work. — *St Francis de Sales (1567-1622)*.

* * *

The primary end of marriage is the procreation and education of children.

THE procreation of children is the first and principal end of marriage. Hence, no one may ever lawfully depart from the due order that that end requires. — *St Francis de Sales (1567-1622)*.

As for those who are married, chastity is very necessary for them, because in their case it does not consist in abstaining altogether, but in exercising self-control. — *St Francis de Sales (1567-1622)*.

SINCE no act proceeding deliberately from the will is indifferent, the marriage act is always either sinful or meritorious in one possessing grace. — *St Thomas Aquinas (1225-74)*.

IF one is led to perform the marriage act, either by the virtue of justice, in order to render the debt, or by the virtue of religion, that children may be procreated for the worship of God, the act is meritorious. — *St Thomas Aquinas (1225-74)*.

EVEN with a lawful wife, the marriage act is unlawful and shameful if the conception of offspring is prevented. That is what Onan, the son of Juda, did, and on that account God put him to death. — *St Augustine (354-430)*.

Nothing God commands is impossible. He expects us to go as far as we can and to pray for the rest, which He will give us.

GOD does not command impossibilities, but by commanding admonishes you to do what you can and to pray for what you cannot, and aids you that you may be able. — *St. Augustine (354-430).*

* * *

PERFECT married life means the complete dedication of the parents for the benefit of their children. — *St Thomas Aquinas (1225-74).*

THE family is the most ancient institution which God founded in Paradise, when He called the first pair of human beings into existence. The first blessing which God gave was for the wellbeing of the family. With family life, the history of the world commences. — *St John Vianney (1786-1859).*

CHRISTIAN fathers and mothers: if you wish to have pious, good children, you must first of yourselves be God-fearing and lead good lives. As the tree, so will the fruit be, says an old proverb, and the Divine Word verifies this. — *St John Vianney (1786-1859).*

CHRISTIAN husband! Imitate St Joseph by beginning your day's work with God, and ending it for Him. Cherish those belonging to you as the holy foster father did Jesus, and be their faithful protector. — *St John Vianney (1786-1859).*

CHRISTIAN wife! Follow in the footsteps of the ideal of all womanhood, the Blessed Mother of God; in joy and in sorrow, she will be your advocate at the throne of her Son. — *St John Vianney (1786-1859).*

What are the duties of parents towards their children?

FATHERS and mothers owe four things to their children: maintenance, instruction, correction and good example. — *St John Baptist de la Salle (1651-1719).*

WHATEVER others may say, I find no sure basis in educating the young save in frequent Confession and Holy Communion. — *St John Bosco (1815-88).*

Do not forget daily prayer; keep holy the Sundays and Holy days, and receive frequently, being well prepared, the Sacraments. When it is possible, say in common the morning and night prayers, and grace before meals. — *St John Vianney (1786-1859).*

TELL the children about God and His Saints. During the holy time of Lent, speak to them of their suffering Saviour. During Paschal time, of His glorious Resurrection. During Christmas time, of His Birth. You will see what a profound impression it will make on the minds of your children. — *St John Vianney (1786-1859).*

The Faith of the Family should be displayed in the home.

To decorate the houses with religious pictures is a custom as old as Christianity itself, for the true Christian has always considered his home as nothing less than a Temple of God, and the religious pictures as means to extend and preserve the spirit of Christianity in the home. — *St John Vianney (1786-1859).*

IN the living room, the place of honour should be given to the crucifix. — *St John Vianney (1786-1859).*

OF course, religious pictures of themselves will not make a family good. Only when they are contemplated upon, are they a practical help to true Christian sentiment, and to a true Christian way of living in the family. — *St John Vianney (1786-1859).*

*   *   *

CHILDREN should be loved for the love of Him who created them, and not for the love of self nor of the children. — *St Catherine of Siena (1347-80).*

HAPPINESS is to be found only in the home where God is loved and honoured, where each one loves, and helps, and cares for the others. — *Blessed Théophane Vénard (1829-61).*

O! WHAT happiness to grow up in the bosom of a truly Christian family. It requires care, a great deal of care, conscientiously to fulfil the obligations of father and mother. The parents are a mirror to their children: and the children constantly look into this mirror. What a consolation it is for you if you can say: I am the father, the mother of a pious child, pleasing to God and man. — *St John Vianney (1786-1859).*

*   *   *

Perhaps the root of all social disturbance can be traced back to disorder in the family.

Today, when the family is assailed on all sides by disrupting influences and moral peril, we can already begin to see the tell-tale litter of broken homes, delinquency, and juvenile crime, evidence of the widespread breakdown of Christian family life.

Where the wrong was, there must be the remedy.

THE reason why our times are so irreligious is on account of the unchristian families. Where the wrong was, there must be the remedy. All the authority of Church and State is useless if the family does not co-operate. — *St John Vianney (1786-1859)*.

DISORDER in society is the result of disorder in the family. — *St Angela Merici (1470-1540)*.

THE prevailing spirit of the household corresponds with the literature in the home. Salacious novels and magazines, newspapers which offend our moral sense, are too often mental food in many homes. Alas, how many hearts have been poisoned in their youth by obscene literature. Do not permit anything of the kind to be brought into your home. — *St John Vianney (1786-1859)*.

We might add also, the growing disregard for Christian moral principles prevalent in the entertainment world.

If the family is to be safeguarded from so many under-mining influences, parents must maintain a constant vigil over their children and guide them away from all that is likely to prove morally harmful.

This duty is delegated to them by God.

THE home must be in accord with the Church, that all harmful influences be withheld from the souls of children. Where there is true piety in the home, purity of morals reigns supreme. — *St John Vianney (1786-1859)*.

IF we wish to see any improvement in the state community or the family, the family must, in common with the Church, educate the children in Christianity. It is true that the hope of a better future is founded on a good, obedient youth. — *St John Vianney (1786-1859)*.

Christ must come into the family!
Christ must remain in the family!
Let this be your motto. Then, with the help of God, a devout, chaste generation will spring up to the joy of the parents and of the Church, the support and consolation of your old age. — *St John Vianney (1786-1859).*

THE FAMILY ROSARY

THE following method of saying the Family Rosary helps us to curb our distractions and reminds us of the mystery we are commemorating.

In order to do this, we must add a word or two to each Hail Mary (depending upon the decade). This word or words should be added after the word "Jesus".

"And blessed is the fruit of thy womb";

At the 1st Decade . . . "Jesus incarnate";
At the 2nd Decade . . . "Jesus sanctifying";
At the 3rd Decade . . . "Jesus born in poverty";
At the 4th Decade . . . "Jesus sacrificed";
At the 5th Decade . . . "Jesus, Saint among saints";
At the 6th Decade . . . "Jesus in His agony";
At the 7th Decade . . . "Jesus scourged";
At the 8th Decade . . . "Jesus crowned with thorns";
At the 9th Decade . . . "Jesus carrying His Cross";
At the 10th Decade . . . "Jesus crucified";
At the 11th Decade . . . "Jesus risen from the dead";
At the 12th Decade . . . "Jesus ascending into Heaven";
At the 13th Decade . . . "Jesus filling thee with the Holy Spirit";
At the 14th Decade . . . "Jesus raising thee up";
At the 15th Decade . . . "Jesus crowning thee".
— *St Louis de Montfort (1673-1716).*

14

GUIDE FOR THE YOUNG

CHRIST made my soul beautiful with the jewels of grace and virtue. I belong to Him whom the angels serve. — *St Agnes (IVth century)*.

* * *

The following pages have been composed specially for the young. They consist of counsels written mostly by child Saints and Saints who were dedicated to the welfare of youth. Many of these selections have been drawn from the wonderful words of advice given by St John Bosco to his boys . . . words that are perhaps even more timely today than when they were written one hundred years ago.

JESUS is the teacher of holiness. I go to Him because I want Him to teach me how to become a Saint. Of what use to me is all I learn in school if I do not become holy? — *St Francis de Sales (in boyhood) (1567-1622)*.

I FEEL a longing and a need to be a Saint. I did not know it was so easy to be one, but now I see that one can be holy and happy too. I feel I simply *must* be a Saint. — *St Dominic Savio (1842-57)*.

Another young Saint expressed the same thought after her first Communion.

I CAN no longer live without Jesus. How soon shall I receive Him again? — *St Maria Goretti (1890-1902)*.

IT is better to be the child of God than king of the whole world. — *St Aloysius Gonzaga (1568-91)*.

OFTEN say to yourself: if I wish to become a Saint, I must suffer. If I wish to please God, I must do His Will and not my own. — *St Alphonsus Liguori (1696-1787)*.

IF I do not become a Saint, I am doing nothing. — *St Dominic Savio (1842-57)*.

The following were the resolutions of St Dominic Savio when he was barely twelve years of age.

I WILL go to Confession and to Communion often.
I will keep holy the feast days.
Jesus will be my best friend.
And I will rather die than commit a sin. — *St Dominic Savio (1842-57)*.

WHEN I am at all worried, I go to my confessor, who shows me what is God's Will; for Jesus Christ Himself assures us that he speaks with the Voice of God. — *St Dominic Savio (1842-57)*.

WHEN I want something important, I go to Holy Communion, where I receive the same Body that our Lord offered up for us on the Cross, together with His Precious Blood, His Soul and His Divinity.

What more is wanting to complete my happiness until the day when I shall see face to face Him whom I now see on our altars only with the eye of faith? — *St Dominic Savio (1842-57)*.

OUR Lord needs from us neither great deeds nor profound thoughts. Neither intelligence nor talents. He cherishes simplicity. — *St Thérèse of Lisieux (1873-97)*.

IT was well that our Lord told us: "*In My Father's house there are many mansions*" (*John 14. 2*). If there are some for great souls, for the Fathers of the desert, and the martyrs of penance, there must also be one for little children.

And in that one, a place is kept for us if we but love Him dearly together with our Father and the Spirit of Love. — *St Thérèse of Lisieux (1873-97)*.

Holiness and happiness go hand in hand, as St Dominic Savio discovered.

LAUGH and play and dash about as much as you like, only be careful not to say or do anything that would be displeasing to God. — *St Mary Mazzarello (1837-81)*.

HAVE love in your hearts, but repress the tendency to appear devout. — *St Mary Mazzarello (1837-81)*.

What are the duties of children towards their parents?

THE first duty of children to their parents is respect at all times, and on all occasions. A father and mother are, in regard to their children, the representatives of God.

To fail in respect towards them, is to fail in respect towards God Himself. — *St John Baptist de la Salle (1651-1719)*.

THE second duty of children is to love their parents. — *St John Baptist de la Salle (1651-1719)*.

THE third duty is obedience. "*Children*," says St Paul, "*obey your parents in the Lord, for this is just*" (*Ephes. 6. 1.*). — *St John Baptist de la Salle (1651-1719)*.

GOD loves obedience better than sacrifice. — *Blessed John Ruysbroeck (1293-1381)*.

* * *

The principal snare endangering the young is idleness. This is the source of all evil.

THE principal trap which the devil sets for the young people is idleness. This is the fatal source of all evil. Do not let there be any doubt in your mind, that man was born to work, and that when he does not do so he is out of his element and in great danger of offending God. — *St John Bosco (1815-88)*.

I DO not mean by this that you should be occupied from morning till night without some recreation. You should be able to find enjoyment in useful hobbies, and also take pleasure in the study of history and geography, the arts and sciences. — *St John Bosco (1815-88)*.

Do you wish to study to your advantage? Let devotion accompany all your studies. Consult God more than your books. Ask Him to make you understand what you read. Never begin or end your study except by prayer. Science is a gift of God. Do not consider it merely the work of your own mind and effort. — *St Vincent Ferrer (1350-1419)*.

WHEN you begin to study, look up to Him and think: 'O Lord, how worthless this knowledge would be, if it were not for the enlightening of my mind for Thy service, or for making me more useful to my fellow men.' — *Blessed Elizabeth Seton (1774-1821)*.

FOR recreation, choose the games which are approved and which also help to make you strong in body. Do not cheat, or upset others, by showing bad temper. Raise your mind sometimes to God, or our Blessed Lady, by means of a little prayer; thus following the advice of St Paul: *Do all for the glory of God.* — *St John Bosco (1815-88)*.

ST ALOYSIUS was once asked, while playing happily with his companions, what he would do if an angel told him that in a quarter of an hour he would die, and have to appear before the judgment seat of God. The Saint promptly replied that he would continue playing, '*because*,' he said, '*I am certain that these games are pleasing to God.*'

I recommend also most earnestly that in your games and recreation you avoid bad companions as you would a dangerous disease. — *St John Bosco (1815-88)*.

Who are bad companions?

THEY are those who in your presence are not ashamed to make use of scandalous words, and expressions of double meaning. Those who grumble, tell lies, swear, blaspheme; those who try to keep you away from church, want you to steal, disobey your parents and superiors, or to neglect your duty.

With tears in my eyes, I beseech you to keep far away from such companions. — *St John Bosco (1815-88)*.

LISTEN to the words of the Holy Spirit: '*He that walks with the wise shall be wise: a friend of fools shall become like to them.*' Fly from bad companions as from the bite of a poisonous snake.

If you keep with good companions, I can assure you that you will one day rejoice with the blessed in Heaven; whereas if you keep with those who are bad, you will become bad yourself, and you will be in danger of losing your soul. — *St John Bosco (1815-88)*.

One of the most difficult virtues for the young to practise is Purity. So many snares have been laid in the path of youth by the corrupt influences of today, that it requires the most constant watch over the senses to evade or overcome them.

KEEP this well in mind. Never read books you are not sure about. Don't read bad books, or those which are not really suitable for your age. Even supposing these bad books are very well written from a literary point of view, let me ask you this: would you drink something you knew was poisoned just because it was offered to you in a golden cup? — *St John Bosco (1815-88).*

THE reading of bad books fills the imagination with bad thoughts. Through the mind the poison passes, and there begets ruin and death. — *St John Baptist de la Salle (1651-1719).*

ONE bad book is capable of corrupting a multitude of young people. Should such a book come into your hands, do not look into it, lest you be tempted to read it. — *St John Baptist de la Salle (1651-1719).*

BOYS and young men should not be over familiar with girls, otherwise the beautiful virtue of Purity will be exposed to danger. A strict watch over our senses is a valuable help to keep pure. — *St John Bosco (1815-88).*

DO not therefore frequent places of amusement, or dances where there is a danger to morals. Above all, guard your eyes, since they are the windows through which sin enters into the soul. Never look curiously on those things which are contrary to modesty, even slightly. — *St John Bosco (1815-88).*

ST Dominic Savio had a great devotion to the Mother of God, and every day did some little mortification in her honour. On his way to school, he never let his eyes rest on any girl, and when asked why, he replied: *"I want to keep them to rest on the beauty of my Mother Mary one day in Heaven."* — *St John Bosco (1815-88).*

* * *

No matter how good food is, if poison is mixed with it, it may cause the death of him who eats it. So it is with conversation. A single bad word, an evil action, an unbecoming joke, is often enough to harm one or more young listeners, and may later on cause them to lose God's grace. — *St John Bosco (1815-88).*

IF those carrying on the bad talk are younger than you, reprove them severely. If they are those whom you cannot speak to in this way, go away from them if you can. If you cannot do this, take no part in what is going on. Repeat meanwhile in your heart: "*My Jesus, mercy, Mary, Help of Christians, pray for me.*" — *St John Bosco (1815-88).*

Scandal is something that should be avoided at all costs.

HE gives scandal who by word or deed gives occasion to others to offend Almighty God. Scandal is a terrible sin, because it robs God of the souls which He created for Heaven, and redeemed with the Precious Blood of Jesus Christ: and it delivers them into the hands of the devil.

Guard yourself well from this danger, and run away from it as you would run away from the devil himself. — *St John Bosco (1815-88).*

ST Dominic Savio did not hesitate to rebuke his companions, to snatch away the indecent papers from their hands, to hurry them away from the man who was trying to corrupt them.

Let him be your inspiration, realizing that you have the same means to make you courageous in doing good as he had. — *St John Bosco (1815-88).*

* * *

Choose your career with care...

IT is most important that you choose your career with care, so that you may really follow the vocation that God has destined for you. No day should pass without some prayer to this end. Often repeat with St Paul: *"Lord, what will You have me to do?"* — *St John Bosco (1815-88).*

A GREAT help to you always will be a great love for, and unlimited confidence in, our Blessed Lady, Help of Christians, Mother of God, and your Mother also. She says to you: *"Whoever is little, let him come to me."* If you will love her, she will shower on you many graces in this life, and be an assurance to you of Heaven hereafter. — *St John Bosco (1815-88).*

* * *

CONQUER yourself and the world lies at your feet. — *St Augustine (354-430).*

PRAYER

O MARY, I wish always to be thy child. I give thee my heart; keep it thine for ever.

O Jesus, O Mary, be always my friends. I pray you both to let me die rather than commit a sin. Amen. — *St Dominic Savio (1842-57).*

15

THE MEANING OF SUFFERING

LET us understand that God is a Physician, and that suffering is a medicine for salvation, not a punishment for damnation. — *St Augustine (353-430).*

* * *

Christ has told us that the way to Heaven is along the strait path and through the narrow gate.

Suffering may be likened to the tug of God's guiding hand to keep us set upon this thorny way.

THE greatest honour God can do a soul is not to give it much, but to ask much of it. — *St Thérèse of Lisieux (1873-97).*

SUFFERING is the very best gift He has to give us. He gives it only to His chosen friends. — *St Thérèse of Lisieux (1873-97).*

WE always find that those who walked closest to Christ were those who had to bear the greatest trials. — *St Teresa of Avila (1515-82).*

PRESENT sorrow and suffering is the way to glory, the way to the kingdom. — *St Bernard (1090-1153).*

YOUR sufferings will provide the means to purchase Heaven. The things that are according to your liking won't. — *Blessed Raphaela Mary (1850-1925).*

SUFFERING is the money with which one buys Heaven. — *Blessed Théophane Vénard (1829-61).*

CAN you expect to go to Heaven for nothing? Did not our dear Saviour track the whole way to it with His Blood and tears? — *Blessed Elizabeth Seton (1774-1821).*

ONE must suffer to gain Eternal Life. — *St Thérèse of Lisieux (1873-97).*

WE *must suffer* in order to go to God. We forget this truth far too often. — *St Madeleine Sophie Barat (1779-1865).*

THE way of the cross by trials suffered for God is the way to Heaven. — *St Alphonsus Rodriguez (1517-71).*

IF there be a true way that leads to the Everlasting Kingdom, it is most certainly that of suffering, patiently endured. — *St Colette (1381-1447).*

WE can only go to Heaven through suffering, but it is not all that suffer who find salvation. It is only those who suffer readily for the love of Jesus Christ, who first suffered for us. — *St Vincent de Paul (1580-1660).*

To those who love more, He gives more suffering. To those who love less, less. — *St Thérèse of Lisieux (1873-97).*

* * *

The Saints have given us a very explicit answer to the hard question: "Why does God make me suffer?"

THE world is bitter and is loved. If it were sweet, how ardently, think you, should it be loved? — *St Augustine (354-430).*

A GREAT servant of God once said that 'if some gall were not mingled in our earthly cup, we should be content with our exile, and think less of our own true country.' — *Blessed Théophane Vénard (1829-61).*

As iron is fashioned by fire and on the anvil, so in the fire of suffering and under the weight of trials, our souls receive that form which our Lord desires them to have. — *St Madeleine Sophie Barat (1779-1865).*

IF God causes you to suffer much, it is a sign that He has great designs for you, and that He certainly intends to make you a Saint. And if you wish to become a great Saint, entreat Him yourself to give you much opportunity for suffering; for there is no wood better to kindle the fire of holy love than the wood of the cross, which Christ used for His own sacrifice of boundless charity. — *St Ignatius Loyola (1491-1556).*

THE sick are to realize that they are sons of God by the very fact that the scourge of discipline chastises them. For unless it were His plan to give them an inheritance after their chastisements, He would not trouble to school them in afflictions. — *St Gregory the Great (d. 604).*

WE must remember that all incapacity and distress is sent to us by God. Life and death, health and sickness, are all ordered by Him; and in whatever form they come, it is always to help us and for our good. — *St Vincent de Paul (1580-1660).*

JESUS Christ teaches you that you will only participate in His consolations in proportion to your constancy in suffering after His example and for His love. — *St Ignatius Loyola (1491-1556).*

WHAT Saint has ever won his crown without first contending for it? — *St Jerome (342-420).*

* * *

THE greatness of our love of God must be tested by the desire we have of suffering for His sake. — *St Philip Neri (1515-95).*

OUR Lord tests the servants He most values, sometimes in one way, and sometimes in another, that they may be put to every sort of proof. — *St Vincent de Paul (1580-1660).*

GOD has many kinds of crosses with which he chastens His friends. — *Blessed Henry Suso (d. 1365).*

No one ought to consider himself a true servant of God who is not tried by many temptations and trials. — *St Francis of Assisi (1181-1226).*

YOU ought to thank God when He chastises you; for His chastisements are a proof that He loves you, and receives you into the number of His children. "*Whoever the Lord loveth,*" says St Paul, "*He chastiseth, and He scourgeth every son whom He receiveth*" *(Heb. 12. 6).* — *St Alphonsus Liguori (1696-1787).*

WHEN God wills you to begin truly to suffer and sends you what you would most avoid suffering, then you may be confident that you are loved by Him and may hope to see the face of the Lord with joy. — *Blessed John of Avila (1500-69).*

IF we have any natural defect, either in mind or body, let us not grieve and be sorry for ourselves.

Who is there that ever receives a gift and tries to make bargains about it? Let us, then, return God thanks for what, through a pure act of His Goodness, He has bestowed upon us, and let us be content with the manner in which He has treated us. Who can tell whether, if we had had a larger share of ability or stronger health, we should not have possessed them to our destruction? — *St Alphonsus Liguori (1696-1787).*

GOD could in no wise permit the kind of evil out of which He could not bring good. — *St Augustine (354-430).*

OUR Lord who saved the world through the Cross, will only work for the good of souls through the Cross. — *St Madeleine Sophie Barat (1779-1865).*

* * *

From these illuminating words, we can begin to understand why it is so necessary for us to accept with submission the sufferings sent by God for our spiritual good.

The Saints counsel us to pray ceaselessly for the fortitude necessary to remain steadfast in every adversity. The hammer blows of pain, the drawn out anguish of bereavement, years of interminable hardship and distress; perhaps, a shattered life, a hopeless morrow. These are the burning darts which a merciful Father aims into the hearts of His loving children.

For He would have us wholly to Himself.

* * *

BEAR the cross and do not make the cross bear you. — *St Philip Neri (1515-95).*

YOU say that you are weak? Have you fathomed the strength of God? — *St Madeleine Sophie Barat (1779-1865)*.

THERE is no purgatory in this world. Nothing but heaven or hell.

Sufferings are a kind of paradise to him who suffers them with patience, while they are a hell to him who has no patience. — *St Philip Neri (1515-95)*.

HE who bears his sufferings with patience for God's sake, will soon arrive at high perfection. He will be master of the world, and will already have one foot in the other world. — *Blessed Giles of Assisi (d. 1262)*.

ONLY one thing is necessary in your anguish: bear everything with resignation to the Divine Will; for this will help you to attain your eternal salvation. Hope with a lively faith and you will receive everything from Almighty God. — *St Gerard Majella (1726-55)*.

* * *

Patience is an indispensable virtue. . .

THE virtue of Patience is the one which most assures us of perfection. — *St Francis de Sales (1567-1622)*.

PATIENCE is the root and guardian of all the virtues. — *St Gregory the Great (d. 604)*.

THE virtue of Patience is so great a gift of God, that we even preach the patience of Him who bestows it upon us. — *St Augustine (354-430)*.

THOSE are patient who would rather bear evils without inflicting them, than inflict them without bearing them. — *St Augustine (354-430)*.

THE prayer of the sick person is his patience and his acceptance of the sickness for the love of Jesus Christ. This has great worth when it is motivated by the imitation of how much He suffered for us, and by penance for our sins. — *St Charles of Sezze (1613-70)*.

PATIENCE is a perfect sacrifice that we can offer to God, because in our trials we do nothing but accept from His hands the cross that He sends us. — *St Alphonsus Liguori (1696-1787)*.

LET nothing disturb you,
Let nothing frighten you,
Though all things pass
God does not change.
Patience wins all things.
But he lacks nothing
Who possesses God;
For God alone suffices. — *St Teresa of Avila (1515-82)*.

THOUGH perseverance does not come from our power, yet it comes within power. — *St Francis de Sales (1567-1622)*.

This truth is movingly borne out in the following burning words uttered by one of the forty English Reformation martyrs undergoing extreme torture for the Faith.

LORD, more pain if Thou pleasest. And more patience. — *Blessed Eustace White (d. 1591)*.

* * *

In the midst of our trials, we must always be resigned to the Will of God.

IN all trials, I will say always: *"Lord, Thy Will be done"*. *St Gerard Majella (1726-55)*.

WE must also be especially resigned in mortal sickness. To accept death at such a time, in order that the Will of God may be fulfilled, merits for us a reward similar to that of the martyrs, because they accepted death to please God. — *St Alphonsus Liguori (1696-1787)*.

And if we refuse to accept the Cross...

WHAT does he gain who refuses the cross? He increases its weight. — *St Alphonsus Liguori (1696-1787)*.

HE who embraces the cross and bears it with patience lightens the weight of the cross. Indeed, the weight itself becomes a consolation; for God abounds with grace to all those who carry the cross with good will in order to please Him. — *St Alphonsus Liguori (1696-1787)*.

BY the law of nature, there is no pleasure in suffering; but Divine Love, when It reigns in a heart, makes it take delight in its sufferings. — *St Alphonsus Liguori (1696-1787)*.

How can you wish to be freed from your sufferings? Do you not yet know that no mortification is so pleasing to God as the joyful, or at least patient acceptance of the crosses He imposes? Fasting, watching, and mortifying the flesh are good kinds of penance, but suffering in union with our suffering Lord and Saviour is incomparably better. — *St Pachomius (292-348)*.

HE who cannot suffer for Jesus Christ does not know how to gain Jesus Christ for his own. — *St Joseph Calasanctius (1556-1648).*

To suffer and not to suffer for God is torment. — *St Gerard Majella (1726-55).*

* * *

The Saints urge us to contemplate the crucifix and unite our sorrows with the sufferings of our Divine Lord.

YOU will have no difficulty in loving the Cross if you think often of the words: *"He loved me and delivered Himself up for me"* (Gal. 2. 20). — *St Thérèse of Lisieux (1873-97).*

THE crosses with which our path through life is strewn associate us with Jesus in the mystery of His crucifixion. — *St John Eudes (1601-80).*

As in Heaven nothing will be sweeter than to resemble Him in His glory, so here on earth, nothing is more to our advantage than to be like Him in His Passion. — *St Robert Bellarmine (1542-1621).*

GOD does us great honour when He is pleased that we should tread the same road which was trodden by His only-begotten Son. — *St Paul of the Cross (1694-1775).*

FOLLOW after Christ and carry your cross for your salvation, as Christ carried His Cross for your salvation. — *St Anthony of Padua (1195-1231).*

IT is suffering that makes us like to Him. — *St Thérèse of Lisieux (1873-97).*

IT is loving the Cross that one finds one's heart, for Divine Love cannot live without suffering. — *St Bernadette (1844-79)*.

WHAT are pain, sorrow, poverty, reproach? Blessed Lord, they all were once Thy chosen companions, and can I reject them as enemies, and fly from the friends Thou sendest to bring me to Thy Kingdom? — *Blessed Elizabeth Seton (1774-1821)*.

KNOW that the experience of pain is something so noble and precious that the Divine Word, who enjoyed the abundant riches of Paradise, yet, because He was not clothed with this ornament of sorrow, came down from Heaven to seek it upon the earth. — *St Mary Magdalen of Pazzi (1566-1607)*.

RECALL to yourself that our Lord is the beloved Son of the living God; that He is Himself the God of all consolation, the sight of whom forms the beatitude of the angels and elect. And yet, what does He not suffer! — *St Ignatius Loyola (1491-1556)*.

LOOK at His adorable Face.
Look at His glazed and sunken eyes.
Look at His wounds.
Look Jesus in the Face.
There, you will see how He loves us. — *St Thérèse of Lisieux (1873-97)*.

LET the crucifix be not only in my eyes and on my breast, but in my heart. — *St Bernadette (1844-79)*.

How can we complain when He Himself was considered *'as one struck by God and afflicted'* (Isa. 53. 4). — *St Thérèse of Lisieux (1873-97)*.

LET us go to the foot of the Cross and there complain—
if we have the courage. — *St Madeleine Sophie Barat
(1779-1865)*.

ALL sufferings, however great, become sweet when we
look at Jesus on the Cross. — *St Mary Magdalen of
Pazzi (1566-1607)*.

Is there anything that a generous heart would not willingly suffer on contemplating Jesus crucified? — *Blessed
Raphaela Mary (1850-1925)*.

O JESUS! Release all my affections and draw them up-
wards. Let my crucified heart sink forever into yours
and bury itself in the mysterious wound made by the
entry of the lance. — *St Bernadette (1844-79)*.

CALVARY is the spot on earth which is nearest to Heaven.
— *St Madeleine Sophie Barat (1779-1865)*.

* * *

LIFE passes. Eternity comes to meet us with great strides.
Soon, we shall be living with the very life of Jesus. Having
drunk deep at the source of all bitterness, we shall be
deified in the very source of all joys, of all delights. —
St Thérèse of Lisieux (1873-97).

LIFE is only a dream: soon, we shall awaken. And what
joy! The greater our sufferings, the more limitless our
glory. Oh! do not let us waste the trial Jesus sends. —
St Thérèse of Lisieux (1873-97).

THE suffering of adversity does not degrade you but
exalts you. Human tribulation teaches you; it does not
destroy you. The more we are afflicted in this world,

the greater is our assurance for the next. The more we sorrow in the present, the greater will be our joy in the future. — *St Isidore of Seville (d. 636)*.

The following lines may still be seen engraved on the wall of a cell in the Tower of London by a Saint who endured the most terrible privations there for ten years, before dying for the Faith.

THE more suffering we endure for Christ in this world, the greater our glory with Him in the next. — *Blessed Philip Howard (d. 1595)*.

WE must often draw the comparison of time and eternity. That is the remedy for all our troubles. How small will the present moment appear when we enter that great ocean! How much we will then wish we had doubled our penances and sufferings while that moment lasted. — *Blessed Elizabeth Seton (1774-1821)*.

THOSE who have not altogether lost their fervour for the spiritual life, can find true happiness nowhere but in the Cross of Christ. All the pleasures of the world seem to them heavy and wearisome when once they have experienced the sweetness of the Saviour's yoke, so that it seems to them a grievous thing if they have no cross to carry, and are left to live without trials and sufferings. — *St Francis Borgia (1510-72)*.

NOTHING more glorious can happen to a Christian than to suffer for Christ. — *St Philip Neri (1515-95)*.

OUR joy depends upon the Cross, and our Lord would not enter into His glory save by the way of bitterness. He leads you by the same path as the Saints. — *St Vincent de Paul (1580-1660)*.

LIFE without a cross is the heaviest cross of all. — *St Sebastian Valfré (1629-1710).*

* * *

IF we endure all things patiently and with gladness, thinking on the sufferings of our Blessed Lord, and bearing all for the love of Him: herein is Perfect Joy. — *St Francis of Assisi (1181-1226).*

ALL suffering is slight to gain Heaven. — *St Joseph Calasanctius (1556-1648).*

ONLY a little more confidence in God. A little more patience. And the end will come, and past weary years will seem as nothing.

Then will arrive the moment of reunion, and all will be amply compensated and repaid, principle and interest. — *Blessed Théophane Vénard (1829-61).*

YOUR reward in Heaven will make up completely for all your pain and suffering. — *St John Bosco (1815-88).*

WHEN we shall see Him in Heaven, then we shall understand the price of suffering and trial.

Like Jesus, we shall say: "*It was truly necessary for suffering to try us and bring us to glory*" (Luke 24. 26) — *St Thérèse of Lisieux (1873-97).*

PRAYER

LORD of all created things, my God, my Blessedness! How long must I yet wait before Thou dost show Thyself to me? How tedious and how full of sufferings is such a life in which one does not really live, but experience on every side utter desolation. How long, O Lord, how long will it yet last? What must I do, my Highest Good? Must I desire, really, to yearn for Thee?

My God and my Creator! Thou dost wound, but Thou dost offer also the balm of healing. Thou dost wound, yet there can be seen no wound. Thou slayest, and Thou grantest life anew. In Thy Omnipotence, according to Thy good Will, Thou disposest, O Lord, of all.

Dost Thou, my God, then will that I, contemptible creature that I am, should endure such tribulation? So be it, then, my God, since Thou dost will it, for my will is Thine. But, O my Creator! the excess of my pain drives me to cry out and bewail my helplessness: may it be Thy good pleasure to relieve me.

The fettered soul yearns for freedom, but wills it no sooner than is pleasing to Thee.

My soul: let then the Will of God be accomplished in thee. Serve the Lord, trust in His Mercy: this will soothe thy pains.

O my God! My King! I can do nothing unless Thy mighty hand, unless Thy heavenly power, assist me.

With Thy help, I can do all. Amen. — *St Teresa of Avila (1515-82)*.

16

LEAN ON GOD

GOD is not a deceiver, that He should offer to support us, and then, when we lean upon Him, should slip away from us. — *St Augustine (354-430)*.

* * *

"*Come to Me*," *pleads our Blessed Saviour*, "*all you that labour and are burdened; I will give you rest. Take My yoke upon yourselves, and learn from Me; I am gentle and humble of Heart; and you shall find rest for your souls.*"

GOD wishes us not to rest upon anything but His infinite Goodness. Do not let us expect anything, hope anything, or desire anything but from Him, and let us put our trust and confidence in Him alone. — *St Charles Borromeo (1538-84)*.

GOD is full of compassion, and never fails those who are afflicted and despised, if they trust in Him alone. — *St Teresa of Avila (1515-82)*.

IN sorrow and suffering, go straight to God with confidence, and you will be strengthened, enlightened and instructed. — *St John of the Cross (1542-91)*.

GOD is faithful, and if we serve Him faithfully, He will provide for our needs. — *St Richard of Chichester (d. 1253)*.

HOPE everything from the Mercy of God. It is as bound-less as His Power. — *St Frances of Rome (1384-1440)*.

WHEN did it ever happen that a man had confidence in God and was lost? *"No one hath hoped in the Lord, and hath been confounded"* (Ecclus. 2. 11). — *St Alphonsus Liguori (1696-1787)*.

MY hope is in Christ, who strengthens the weakest by His Divine help. I can do all in Him who strengthens me. His Power is infinite, and if I lean on Him, it will be mine. His Wisdom is infinite, and if I look to Him for counsel, I shall not be deceived. His Goodness is infinite, and if my trust is stayed on Him, I shall not be abandoned. — *St Pius X (1835-1914)*.

★   ★   ★

The more we set our trust in God, the more we will receive from Him.

ALL things upon which you set your trust are yours. Do but expect much of God, and He will do much for you. Expect but little, and He will do little. — *St Bernard (1090-1153)*.

THE greater and more persistent your confidence in God, the more abundantly you will receive all that you ask. — *St Albert the Great (d. 1280)*.

WE can never have too much hope in God. He gives in the measure we ask. — *St Thérèse of Lisieux (1873-97)*.

IF I saw the gates of Hell open and I stood on the brink of the abyss, I should not despair, I should not lose hope

of mercy, because I should trust in Thee, my God. —
St Gemma Galgani (1878-1903).

* * *

*The Saints warn us against the dangers of presumption.
If we are carried away by self-confidence at the expense
of God, we are lost.*

NEVER trust to yourself, either on the ground of experience, or length of time, or age, or sickness; but always
fly from every occasion of danger as long as you have
strength to raise your eyelids. — *St Philip Neri
(1515-95).*

THERE is great reason you should distrust yourself, but
there is much greater reason that you should trust
yourself entirely to your Divine Saviour. — *St Vincent
de Paul (1580-1660).*

HE who trusts in himself is lost. He who trusts in God
can do all things. — *St Alphonsus Liguori (1696-1787).*

IF hope goes it alone, it ought to be called presumption.
— *St Laurence Justinian (1381-1455).*

PRESUMPTION is the highway to ruin. — *St Jerome
(342-420).*

What grounds have we for trusting in our own capabilities?

HOPE not in thyself, but in thy God. For if thou hopest
in thyself, thy soul is troubled within thee, since it hath
not yet found that whereby it may be confident concerning thee. — *St Augustine (354-430).*

DISTRUST of our own capacity is the foundation for the right sort of confidence in God. — *St Vincent de Paul (1580-1660)*.

*   *   *

Let us cast all our care on God, for He cares for us.

WAIT upon the Lord: wait upon Him patiently, wait upon Him by avoiding all sin. He will come; doubt it not. To this firm hope, join the practice of virtue, and even in this life you will begin to taste the ineffable joys of Paradise. — *St Bernard (1090-1153)*.

WHEN we have once placed ourselves entirely in the hands of God, we need fear no evil. If adversity comes, He knows how to turn it to our advantage, by means which will in time be made clear to us. — *St Vincent de Paul (1580-1660)*.

Do not look forward to what may happen tomorrow.
The same Eternal Father who cares for you today
Will take care of you tomorrow
And every day of your life.
He will either shield you from suffering,
Or He will give you unfailing strength to bear it.
Be at peace, then, and put aside all anxious thoughts. —
St Francis de Sales (1567-1622).

TRUST the past to the Mercy of God, the present to His Love, and the future to His Providence. — *St Augustine (354-430)*.

PRAYER

O SWEETEST Lord Jesus Christ, may my soul ever yearn towards Thee: may my soul seek Thee, find Thee, tend towards attainment of Thee, ever meditate on Thee, and do all things to the praise and glory of Thy Holy Name.

Do Thou alone be my hope, my whole trust, my delight, my joy, my rest, my peace and my sweet contentment.

Do Thou alone be my refuge and my help, my wisdom and my possession, my treasure in whom my heart and my soul may remain fixed immovably, forever. Amen.
— *St Bonaventure (1221-74)*.

17

BEHOLD THY MOTHER

Our Lady's love is like a limpid stream that has its source in the Eternal Fountains, quenches the thirst of all, can never be drained, and ever flows back to its Source. — *Blessed Margaret Bourgeoys (1620-1700).*

* * *

Down through the ages, the Saints have vied with each other in singing the praises of Mary, the Mother of God and the Mother of men.

To the modern world, she is, perhaps, best represented as an intercessor between God and man. During her recent apparitions at Fatima, Portugal, in 1917, we see her in the role of peacemaker—pleading with us to pray and do penance and return to her Divine Son and thus spare the world from the horrors of nuclear war.

"If men do what I ask, there will be peace in the world and Russia will be converted."

The lines below give eloquent testimony to her maternal concern for every member of the human family.

"*Behold thy Mother*" *(John 19. 26).* By these words Mary, by reason of the love she bore them, became the Mother, not only of St John, but of all men. — *St Bernardine of Siena (1380-1444).*

134

MARY was raised to the dignity of Mother of God rather for sinners than for the just, since Jesus Christ declares that He came to call not the just, but sinners. — *St Anselm (1033-1109)*.

ALTHOUGH in the most pure womb of Mary there was but one grain of corn which was Jesus Christ, yet it is called a heap of wheat, because all the elect were virtually contained in it. — *St Ambrose (340-97)*.

SHE is truly our Mother; not indeed carnally, but spiritually; of our souls and of our salvation. For she, by giving us Jesus, gave us true life; and afterwards, by offering the life of her Son on Calvary for our salvation, she brought us forth to the life of grace. — *St Alphonsus Liguori (1696-1787)*.

WE are exceedingly dear to Mary on account of the suffering we cost her. Mothers generally love those children most, the preservation of whose lives has cost them the most suffering. We are those children for whom Mary, in order to obtain for us the life of grace, was obliged to endure the bitter agony of herself offering her beloved Jesus to die before her own eyes, of the most cruel torments. — *St Alphonsus Liguori (1696-1787)*.

SHE seeks for those who approach her devoutly and with reverence, for such she loves, nourishes, and adopts as her children. — *St Bonaventure (1221-74)*.

LET us then cast ourselves at the feet of this good Mother, and embracing them, let us not depart until she blesses us, and accepts us for her children. — *St Bernard (1090-1153)*.

* * *

The Mother of God is also the Queen of Heaven.

IF the Son is a King, the Mother who begot Him is rightly and truly considered a Queen and Sovereign. — *St Athanasius (297-373).*

SHE is a Queen so sweet, so merciful and so ready to help us in our sorrows, that Holy Church wills that we should salute her under the title of Queen of Mercy. — *St Alphonsus Liguori (1696-1787).*

No sooner had Mary consented to be Mother of the Eternal Word, than she merited by this consent to be made Queen of the world and of all creatures. — *St Bernardine of Siena (1380-1444).*

BUT perhaps, now that you are raised to the high dignity of Queen of Heaven, you will forget us poor creatures? Ah, far be such a thought from our minds, for it would little become the great compassion that reigns in the Heart of Mary ever to forget such misery as ours. — *St Peter Damian (1007-72).*

* * *

More than ever, in these sombre times through which we are passing, we feel the need of her protection—like that of an anxious child for the shelter and safety of its mother's arms.

TRULY we are passing through disastrous times, when we may well make our own the lamentation of the Prophet: *"There is no truth, and there is no mercy, and there is no knowledge of God in the land"* (Osee 4. 1) Yet in the midst of this tide of evil, the Virgin Most Merciful rises before our eyes like a rainbow, as the arbiter of peace between God and man. — *St Pius X (1835-1914)*.

LET the storm rage and the sky darken—not for that shall we be dismayed. If we trust as we should in Mary, we shall recognize in her, the Virgin Most Powerful *"who with virginal foot did crush the head of the serpent."* — *St Pius X (1835-1914)*.

A GENTLE maiden having lodged a God in her womb, asks as its price, peace for the world, salvation for those who are lost, and life for the dead. — *St Peter Chrysolorus (d. 450)*.

Oh HOW long since would the world have been destroyed, had not Mary sustained it by her powerful intercession.
    St Fulgentius (468-533).

Centuries after these words were written, they found a living echo in the words of Mary herself at La Salette in 1846.
    "How long a time do I suffer for you! If I would not have my Son abandon you, I am compelled to pray to Him without ceasing."

THE prayers of His Mother are a pleasure to the Son, because He desires to grant all that is granted on her account, and thus recompense her for the favour she did Him in giving Him His Body. — *St Theophilus (IXth century?)*.

If our life were not under Mary's protection, we might tremble for our perseverance and salvation. — *St Peter Julian Eymard (1811-68)*.

* * *

The Heart of Mary is filled with maternal compassion for her strayed children. . .

THE heart of Mary is the court where the assizes of mercy are held. — *St Madeleine Sophie Barat (1779-1865).*

EVEN whilst living in this world, the heart of Mary was so filled with tenderness and compassion for men, that no one ever suffered so much for his own pains as Mary suffered for the pains of others. — *St Jerome (342-420).*

THE Blessed Virgin has so merciful a heart, that she deserves not only to be called merciful, but mercy itself. — *St Leo the Great (d. 461).*

MARY has made herself all to all, and opens her merciful heart to all, that all may receive of her fullness: the sick, health; those in affliction, comfort; the sinner, pardon; and God, glory. — *St Bernard (1090-1153).*

IT is not without reason that Holy Church, in the words of Ecclesiasticus, calls Mary '*the Mother of holy hope*' (*Ecclus. 24. 24*). She is the mother who gives birth to holy hope in our hearts; not to the vain and transitory goods of this life, but of the eternal rewards of Heaven. — *St Alphonsus Liguori (1696-1787).*

THIS Mother of Mercy has so great a desire to save the most abandoned sinners, that she herself goes in search of them, in order to help them; and if they have recourse to her, she knows how to find the means to render them acceptable to God. — *St Alphonsus Liguori (1696-1787)*

NOR should the multitude of our sins diminish our confidence that Mary will grant our petitions when we cast ourselves at her feet. She is the Mother of Mercy; bu mercy would not be needed did none exist who require it. — *St Alphonsus Liguori (1696-1787)*.

As by Mary, heavenly peace was once for all given to the world, so by her are sinners still reconciled to God. — *St Epiphanius (310-403)*.

THERE is no sinner in the world, however much he may be at enmity with God, who does not return to Him and recover His grace, if he has recourse to her and asks her assistance. — *St Bridget of Sweden (1304-73)*.

BY the prayers of Mary, almost innumerable sinners are converted. — *St Methodius (d. 847)*.

O SINNER, be not discouraged, but have recourse to Mary in all your necessities. Call her to your assistance, for such is the Divine Will that she should help in every kind of necessity. — *St Basil (329-79)*.

O SINNER, whoever you are—grown old in sin, imbedded in wickedness, despair not. Thank your Lord, who, that He might show you mercy, has not only given His Son for your advocate, but, to encourage you to greater confidence, has provided you with a mediatrix, who, by her prayers obtains whatever she wills.

Go then, have recourse to Mary, and you will be saved. — *St Bernard (1090-1153)*.

MOST certainly God will not condemn those sinners who have recourse to Mary, and for whom she prays, since He Himself commended them to her as her children. — *St Alphonsus Liguori (1696-1787)*.

HOWEVER great a sinner may have been, if he shows himself devout to Mary, he will never perish. — *St Hilary (d. 368)*.

How can we fail to be attracted to her who is so attracted to us?

ALL generations shall call thee blessed, because thou hast given life and glory to all nations. — *St Bernard (1090-1153).*

WE praise her virginity, we admire her humility; but because we are poor sinners, mercy attracts us more and tastes sweeter. We embrace mercy more lovingly; we remember it more often, and invoke it more earnestly. — *St Bernard (1090-1153).*

WHO can ever form an idea of the tender care that this most loving Mother takes of all of us, offering and dispensing her mercy to every one. — *St Antoninus (1389-1459).*

IF I love Mary, I am certain of perseverance, and shall obtain whatever I wish from God. — *St John Berchmans (1599-1621).*

* * *

Let it not be said that in placing our hope in her we are confiding in one who is, ultimately, a mere creature.

THOSE who place their hopes in creatures alone are most certainly cursed by God, as the prophet Jeremias says *(Jer. 17. 5).*
   But those who hope in Mary, as Mother of God, who is able to obtain graces and eternal life for them, are truly blessed and acceptable to the heart of God. — *St Alphonsus Liguori (1696-1787).*

Oh, HOW many who were once proud have become humble by devotion to Mary! How many who were passionate have become gentle! How many in the midst of darkness have found light! How many who were in despair have found confidence! How many who were lost have found salvation by the same powerful means. — *St Alphonsus Liguori (1696-1787).*

I AM satisfied that whoever has had recourse to thee, O Blessed Virgin, in his wants, and can remember that he did so in vain, should no more speak of or praise thy mercy. — *St Bernard (1090-1153).*

SHE is my greatest security; she is the source of all my hope. — *St Bernard (1090-1153).*

IF Mary is for us, who shall be against us? — *St Antoninus (1389-1459).*

THE great, the special privilege of Mary is, that she is all-powerful with her Son.

Therefore let us be certain that as her power with God exceeds that of all the Saints, so is she in the same proportion our most loving advocate and the one who is the most solicitous for our welfare. — *St Bonaventure (1221-74).*

★ ★ ★

LET us run to her, and, as her little children, cast ourselves into her arms with a perfect confidence. — *St Francis de Sales (1567-1622).*

HAVING confidence in you, O Mother of God, I shall be saved. Being under your protection, I shall fear nothing. With your help I shall give battle to my enemies and put them to flight; for devotion to you is an arm of salvation. — *St John Damascene (690-749).*

SHE has given us so many proofs that she cares for us like a Mother. — *St Thérèse of Lisieux (1873-97).*

IN dangers of sinning, when assailed by temptations, when doubtful as to how you should act, remember that Mary can help you, and if you but call upon her, she will instantly help you. — *St Alphonsus Liguori (1696-1787).*

THE most sweet name of Mary is a precious ointment, which breathes forth the odour of Divine grace. Let this ointment of salvation enter the inmost recesses of our souls. — *St Anselm (1033-1109).*

TAKE shelter under our Lady's mantle, and do not fear. She will give you all you need. She is very rich, and besides is so very generous with her children. So take advantage without fear and with complete confidence, whenever you need anything. She loves giving. — *Blessed Raphaela Mary (1850-1925).*

★   ★   ★

Mary is the Mediatrix of all graces...

JESUS is the only Mediator of justice who can ask in His own name, and in consideration of His own merits and His own rights. Mary herself obtains what she asks only through the merits of the Saviour, and in virtue of prayer made in the name of Jesus Christ. — *St Bernard (1090-1153).*

NEVERTHELESS, such is the order freely determined by God, that Mary's mediation always intervenes in the dispensation of grace. This order admirably restores the plan vitiated and destroyed by sin; for as a man and a woman concurred in our loss, a man and a woman ought to labour together to redeem us. — *St Bernard (1090-1153)*.

JESUS Christ is the only Mediator of justice, and that by His merits He obtains for us all graces and salvation; but Mary is the mediatrix of grace, because she prays and asks for it in the name of Jesus Christ. — *St Alphonsus Liguori (1696-1787)*.

AS every mandate of grace that is sent by a king passes through the palace gates, so does every grace that comes from Heaven to the world pass through the hands of Mary. — *St Bernard (1090-1153)*.

MARY was given to the world as an aqueduct, by which God's graces incessantly flow to the earth. What honour, what love does not our Lord oblige us to render her, since He has filled her with the plenitude of all good in such a way that, if we have some chance of salvation, we have it all from Mary. — *St Bernard (1090-1153)*.

GOD wills that we should have nothing that has not passed through the hands of Mary. — *St Bernard (1090-1153)*.

ALL the gifts, virtues and graces of the Holy Ghost are distributed by Mary, to whom she wishes, when she wishes, the way she wishes, and as much as she wishes. — *St Bernardine of Siena (1380-1444)*.

No one can be filled by the thought of God except by the Blessed Virgin. — *St Germanus (d. 448)*.

THIS is the Will of God, who wished us to have all things through Mary. If, therefore, there is in us any hope, any grace, and salutary gift, we know it comes to us through her. — *St Bernard (1090-1153)*.

* * *

And finally, we receive Christ Himself from her loving hands.

GOD could have given us the Redeemer of the human race, and the Founder of the Faiths in another way than through the Virgin, but since Divine Providence has been pleased that we should have the Man-God through Mary, who conceived Him by the Holy Ghost and bore Him in her womb, it only remains for us to receive Christ from the hands of Mary. — *St Pius X (1835-1914)*.

IT was through the most holy Virgin Mary that Jesus came into the world, and it is also through her that He has to reign in the world. — *St Louis de Montfort (1673-1716)*.

LET the soul of Mary be in each of us to magnify the Lord, and the spirit of Mary be in each of us to rejoice in God. — *St Ambrose (340-97)*.

THOU wast pre-ordained in the mind of God, above all creatures, that thou mightest beget God Himself in man. — *St Bernardine of Siena (1380-1444)*.

* * *

REJOICE, my soul, and be glad in her; for many good things are prepared for those who praise her. — *St Bonaventure (1221-74)*.

SHE is the stairway to Heaven, and the gate of Paradise. — *St Laurence Justinian (1381-1455)*.

LET us not imagine that we obscure the glory of the Son by the praise we lavish on the Mother; for the more she is honoured, the greater is the glory of her Son. — *St Bernard (1090-1153)*.

YOU never think of Mary without Mary's thinking of God for you. You never praise or honour Mary without Mary's praising and honouring God with you. If you say '*Mary*,' she says '*God*'. St Elizabeth praised Mary, and called her blessed, because she had believed. Mary, the faithful echo of God, at once intoned: "*My soul doth magnify the Lord*" (*Luke 1. 46*). — *St Louis de Montfort (1673-1716)*.

THAT which is given to the Mother redounds to the Son; the honour given to the Queen is honour bestowed on the King. — *St Ildephonsus (d. 667)*.

SHE has given more glory to God than all the Angels and Saints have given Him or ever will give Him. — *St Louis de Montfort (1673-1716)*.

* * *

THE gates of Heaven will open to all who confide in the protection of Mary. — *St Bonaventure (1221-74)*.

O SWEET name, which gives the sinner strength and the blessed hope. We pray you, our Lady, Star of the Sea, shine upon us in our distress on the sea of life, and lead us to safe harbour and the ineffable joys of eternity. — *St Anthony of Padua (1195-1231)*.

As sailors are guided by a star to the port, so are Christians guided to Heaven by Mary. — *St Thomas Aquinas (1225-74)*.

FOLLOWING her, thou canst not wander;
Whilst thou prayest to her thou canst not be without hope;
As long as thou thinkest of her thou wilt be in the path.
Thou canst not fall when she sustains thee;
Thou hast nothing to fear while she protects thee;
If she favour thy voyage, thou wilt reach the harbour of safety without weariness. — *St Bernard (1090-1153)*.

PRAYER

O HOLY Mary! my Mother; into thy blessed trust and special custody, and into the bosom of thy mercy, I this day, and every day, and in the hour of my death, commend my soul and my body. To thee I commit all my anxieties and sorrows, my life and the end of my life, that by thy most holy intercession, and by thy merits, all my actions may be directed and governed by thy will and that of thy Son. Amen. — *St Aloysius Gonzaga (1568-91)*.

EPILOGUE

MAKE up your mind to become a Saint. — *St Mary Mazzarello (1837-81)*.

YOU cannot be half a Saint. You must be a whole Saint or no Saint at all. — *St Thérèse of Lisieux (1873-97)*.

NOTHING is impossible to those who will and those who love. — *St Pius X (1835-1914)*.

IF it were given a man to see virtue's reward in the next life, he would occupy his intellect, memory and will in nothing but good works—careless of danger or fatigue. — *St Catherine of Genoa (1447-1510)*.

BLESSED are they who ardently crave sanctity, for their desire shall be fulfilled. — *St Vincent Pallotti (1795-1850)*.

GOD is so good and merciful, that to obtain Heaven it is sufficient to ask it of Him from our hearts. — *St Benedict Joseph Labré (1748-83)*.

HE who truly desires Love, seeks it truly.
And he who truly seeks it, surely finds it.
And he who finds it has found the Fountain of Life. — *St Francis de Sales (1567-1622)*.

BENEDICAT et custodiat nos omnipotens et misericors Dominus, Pater, et Filius, et Spiritus Sanctus. Amen.

ACKNOWLEDGMENTS

THE Editor wishes to express his grateful acknowledgments and thanks to the following translators, publishers and publications for permission to use the material indicated.

Benziger Brothers, Inc., for permission to quote from the *Summa* of St Thomas Aquinas, translated by the Fathers of the English Dominican Province. Copyright 1947 by Benziger Brothers, Inc., New York.

Burns & Oates Ltd., for permission to quote from *The Way of Perfection* by St Teresa of Avila, translated by a Benedictine of Stanbrook Abbey. All rights reserved by Burns & Oates Ltd., London. Also *Christian Perfection* by Alphonsus Rodriguez published by Burns & Oates Ltd., London.

Doubleday & Company, Inc., for permission to quote from *St Thérèse of Lisieux*, translated by John Beevers. Copyright © 1957 by Doubleday & Company Inc.

Faber & Faber Ltd., for permission to quote from *Selected Writings of St Peter Damian* and *The Ladder of Divine Perfection* by St John Climacus, translated by Patricia McNulty. All rights reserved by Faber & Faber Ltd., London.

Farrar, Straus & Company, Inc., for all the quotations from St Bernadette. From *Bernadette and Lourdes* by Michel de Saint Pierre, translated by Edward Fitzgerald. Copyright 1954 by Farrar, Straus and Company, Inc.

Franciscan Herald Press for permission to quote from *St Anthony* by Sophronius Clasen O.F.M., translated by Ignatius Brady. Copyright 1951 by the Franciscan Herald Press, Chicago.

Harper & Row, for permission to quote from *Introduction to the Devout Life* by St Francis de Sales, edited and newly translated by John K. Ryan. Copyright 1950 by Harper & Row, Publishers, Incorporated.

Henry Regnery Company for permission to quote from the Sermons of the *Curé of Ars* translated by Una Morrissey. Copyright 1960 by Henry Regnery Company, Publishers, Chicago.

Montfort Publications for permission to quote from *True Devotion to Jesus through Mary* by St Louis de Montfort, translated by Rev. F.W. Faber D.D. Copyright 1941 by the Fathers of the Company of Mary. Also, *The Secret of the Rosary* by St Louis de Montfort, translated by Mary Barbour, T.O.P., published by Montfort Fathers Publications.

Sheed & Ward Ltd., London, for permission to quote from the *Collected Letters of St Thérèse of Lisieux* translated by F.J. Sheed. Copyright 1949 by Sheed & Ward Ltd., London.

Joseph F. Wagner, Inc., for permission to quote from the *Sermons of the Curé of Ars* published by Joseph F. Wagner, Inc., New York.

Rev. Claude Williamson for permission to quote from *Letters from the Saints*, published by Rockcliffe, and copyrighted by Rev. Claude Williamson.

The Editor also wishes to thank the following for permission to use the material indicated.

Very Reverend Father Provincial, C.SS.R., New York, for permission to quote from the complete works of St Alphonsus Liguori.

Very Reverend Father Provincial, S.D.B., London, for permission to quote from the *Companion of Youth* by St John Bosco.

Reverend John Gartner, S.S.S., for permission to

quote from *The Real Presence, Our Lady of the Blessed Sacrament* by St Peter Julian Eymard. Also, the *Life of St Peter Julian Eymard* copyright by Blessed Sacrament Fathers, New York, 1962.

Reverend John Gaynor for permission to quote from the *Life of St Vincent Pallotti*, by Rev. John Gaynor, S.C.A., copyright by Society of Catholic Apostolate, 1962.

Mother Seton Guild for permission to quote from *Mother Seton, Mother of many Daughters*, copyright by Mother Seton Guild.

Putnam's & Coward-McCann, for permission to quote from *Saints at Prayer*, copyright by Raymond E.F. Larsson, editor, and published by Coward-Mc-Cann, Inc., New York, 1942.

P.J. Kenedy & Sons, New York, and Burns & Oates, London, for permission to quote from *Butler's Lives of the Saints*, copyright 1901: *Spirit of the Spanish Mystics* by Kathleen Pond, copyright 1958: and *The Way of St Alphonsus Liguori*, by Barry Ulanov, copyright 1961, by P.J. Kenedy & Sons, New York.

The quotations from Holy Scripture are taken from the Douay and Knox translations for which grateful acknowledgment is made to Burns & Oates Ltd.

If you have enjoyed this book, consider making your next selection from among the following . . .

Raised from the Dead. *Fr. Hebert* 15.00
Autobiography of St. Margaret Mary 4.00
Thoughts and Sayings of St. Margaret Mary 3.00
The Voice of the Saints. *Comp. by Francis Johnston* 5.00
The 12 Steps to Holiness and Salvation. *St. Alphonsus* . . 7.00
The Rosary and the Crisis of Faith. *Cirrincione/Nelson* . . 1.25
Sin and Its Consequences. *Cardinal Manning* 5.00
Fourfold Sovereignty of God. *Cardinal Manning* 5.00
Catholic Apologetics Today. *Fr. Most* 8.00
Dialogue of St. Catherine of Siena. Transl. *Thorold* 9.00
Catholic Answer to Jehovah's Witnesses. *D'Angelo* 8.00
Twelve Promises of the Sacred Heart. (100 cards) 5.00
St. Aloysius Gonzaga. *Fr. Meschler* 10.00
The Love of Mary. *D. Roberto* 7.00
Begone Satan. *Fr. Vogl* 2.00
The Prophets and Our Times. *Fr. R. G. Culleton* 11.00
St. Therese, The Little Flower. *John Beevers* 4.50
Mary, The Second Eve. *Cardinal Newman* 2.50
Devotion to Infant Jesus of Prague. Booklet 75
The Faith of Our Fathers. *Cardinal Gibbons* 13.50
The Wonder of Guadalupe. *Francis Johnston* 6.00
Apologetics. *Msgr. Paul Glenn* 9.00
Baltimore Catechism No. 1 . . . . 3.00
Baltimore Catechism No. 2 . . . . 4.00
Baltimore Catechism No. 3 . . . . 7.00
An Explanation of the Baltimore Catechism. *Kinkead* . . . 13.00
Bible History. *Schuster* 10.00
Blessed Eucharist. *Fr. Mueller* 13.00
Catholic Catechism. *Fr. Faerber* 5.00
The Devil. *Fr. Delaporte* 5.00
Dogmatic Theology for the Laity. *Fr. Premm* 18.00
Evidence of Satan in the Modern World. *Cristiani* 8.50
Fifteen Promises of Mary. (100 cards) 5.00
Life of Anne Catherine Emmerich. 2 vols. *Schmoger* 37.50
Life of the Blessed Virgin Mary. *Emmerich* 15.00
Prayer to St. Michael. (100 leaflets) 5.00
Prayerbook of Favorite Litanies. *Fr. Hebert* 9.00
Preparation for Death. (Abridged). *St. Alphonsus* 7.00
Purgatory Explained. *Schouppe* 13.50
Purgatory Explained. (pocket, unabr.). *Schouppe* 7.50
Spiritual Conferences. *Tauler* 12.00
Trustful Surrender to Divine Providence. *Bl. Claude* 4.00
Wife, Mother and Mystic. *Bessieres* 7.00
The Agony of Jesus. *Padre Pio* 1.50

At your bookdealer or direct from the publisher.

Prices guaranteed through December 31, 1994.